I0488734

EUROPEAN UNION
AT A GLANCE

Statistical portrait with innovative table-graphs for 30 selected indicators over 28 countries in time perspective

PAVLE SICHERL

Gaptimer Report No. 3

Copyright © 2014 Pavle Sicherl

Ljubljana, May 2014

Layout and Figures: Jaka Hajnšek

Printed by CreateSpace, An Amazon.com Company.

ISBN 978-1499292220

FOREWORD

European Union at a Glance presents an easily understandable overview of 30 selected indicators over 28 EU countries in time, being probably the most condensed summary picture of disparities and dynamics in the EU over many domains over time.

This Gaptimer Report No. 3 is timely publication very useful for discussion of the situation in the EU in light of the forthcoming new European Commission and European Parliament and at the occasion of the 10th Anniversary of the largest EU expansion in 2004.

Its two main characteristics are the innovative table-graphs for visual presentation of the 30 selected indicators over 28 countries in time, on the one hand, and selection of indicators from many domains in the spirit of Beyond GDP initiatives, on the other.

Time and money are two most important comparators in modern society. Time distance is an innovative approach for looking at time series data. Expressed in time units, the approach is easy to understand and provides a useful complement to existing methods. The time distance approach compares time series in the horizontal dimension, i.e. for a given level of the variable, based on two novel generic statistical measures: S-time-distance and S-time-step. These measures can be derived also from a time matrix that summarises information and that provides a first-level visualization tool. It is this innovative time matrix presentation that enables condensed summary visual presentation over many countries and over time. Secondly, 30 selected indicators from many Eurostat indicators systems like Quality of life; Sustainable Development Indicators, Headline Indicators, Digital Agenda, etc. follow the orientation of Beyond GDP. Time distance method can contribute also to the two of the EU projects: e-Frame and BrainPool.

The 30 time matrices give rich food for thought and imaginative readers can find numerous comparisons and stories in the material. One of them is that the damage done to EU countries by the world financial crisis is much greater when for 28 countries we look also at employment, investment share, risk of poverty, income distribution, health, etc. rather than at GDP alone.

Ljubljana, May 2014   Pavle Sicherl

TABLE OF CONTENTS

INTRODUCTION

Better governance needs many things but also better data and tools for fact based decision making. The art of handling different views of data is crucial for discovering the relevant patterns and for providing a broader framework for policy and business analysis. Sustainable development is by definition a long-run and multi-dimensional phenomenon. Semantics of discussing the issues, in setting the targets and in the implementation should not be based only on static measures; it needs to be complemented by dynamic measures.

One way of presenting and visualising of the time series data for 30 indicators listed below is the time matrix as an innovative complementary approach for looking at time series data. The time matrix provides a good summary overview over many units and years and also a first-level visualisation tool.

Time matrix is an original possibility of additional presentation of time series data. In the usual time series table data of the indicator (e.g. life expectancy) are organised in relation to the descriptors, like units (e.g. countries) and time (e.g. years). The time matrix presents the original data (or some approximations) in an alternative way: descriptors are units and levels of the indicator and the value in the field of the table are times when such levels were attained. Calculating these times by interpolations may pose a small problem of the degree of accuracy compared to the original data, but it offers additional understanding about the time dimension of disparities and a good summary overview.

It is defined for selected levels of a given variable and shows in which year various units (countries, regions, etc.) achieved these levels. The first example of time matrix for indictor 1 life expectancy below condenses information for the period of more than 50 years (1960-2012), which in the Eurostat extended database amounts to more than 1000 entries; in this time matrix it is condensed to much smaller number of entries (228), i.e. nearly five times smaller. This presents a first level visualisation that usefully complements the details in the original database by showing the easily understandable summary dynamic overview.

In short, time distance concept organises the same data from Eurostat databases in a way that data are arranged by selected levels of indicators showing in which year these levels of the indicators were achieved by given country. The result is a LEVEL-TIME MATRIX, which is easily understood by everybody.

One can immediately observe several stories:

1. The observed level-time table-graph in yellow colour shows the range of values achieved for a given country over the period from available data.

This allows for a quick level comparison for time matrices for all 30 indicators:

- vertically comparing levels between countries shows the situation and disparities across the EU countries over time

- comparing horizontally in the row for each country shows how many steps over levels of indicators were achieved (which is an additional indication of the dynamics in the country)

2. Technical comments important for understanding (see also ANNEX with available software Time Matrix Calculator to calculate time matrix from your own data).

The year presented in **bold** show the latest presented year of the indicator for the given country. It can help to quickly observe whether there was a noticeable decrease in the observed period. Technically, if there are more intersections for a given level of the indicator the last year is shown.

As shown below, a time matrix condenses time series information in much smaller number of entries, which is a great advantage for presentation. Statistical offices of international organisations as well as national statistical offices could also use the time matrix presentation to complement their usual time series data tables covering many years and units. By itself (i.e. even without calculating the two new generic statistical measures S-time-distance and S-time-step as shown in matrices 1a, 1b, 2a, and 2b) it can be used in publications, web pages and other software as a first-level visualisation tool to 'turn statistics into knowledge'. The time matrix allows an introductory visualisation of what issues and hypothesis could be best suited for presentation through other visualisation tools such as OECD eXplorer, Google Public Data Explorer and Gapminder.

S-time-matrix can be also used as one possibility of deriving values of S-time-distance and S-time-step as shown in examples 1a and 2a for time distance and 1b and 2b for time step. In these cases S-time-distance between two series can be derived by subtracting vertically the respective times for a given level in the time matrix. Conversely, subtracting the years in the time matrix for consecutive levels of the variable for each row horizontally allows deriving the S-time-step.

A VISUAL OVERVIEW OF DEVELOPMENT IN ALL CURRENT EUROPEAN UNION COUNTRIES BASED ON TIME DISTANCE METHODOLOGY

List of 30 selected indicators

	Indicators	Data range	Top country (last year)
1	Life expectancy at birth	1960-2012	Spain
2	Human Development Index	1980-2012	Netherlands
3	GDP per capita in PPS	1995-2012	Luxembourg
4	Median income in PPS	1995-2013	Luxembourg
5	Employment rate (15 to 64 years)	1992-2012	Netherlands
6	Activity rate (15 to 64 years)	1992-2012	Sweden
7	Share of gross fixed investment in GDP	1954-2013	Estonia
8	R&D expenditure (GERD), percent of GDP	1981-2012	Finland
9	Summary Innovation Index	2008-2012	Sweden
10	Tertiary attainment for age group 15-64	2000-2013	Ireland
11	Proportion of population aged 65 years and more	1961-2013	Italy
12	Old age dependency ratio, projections 2013-2080	2013-2080	Slovakia
13	Population growth rates, total	1961-2013	Luxembourg
14	Persons killed in road accidents per million inhabitants	1990-2012	United Kingdom
15	Death due to homicide, standardised death rate by 100 000 inh.	1994-2010	United Kingdom
16	Infant mortality rate	1960-2012	Slovenia
17	At-risk-of-poverty (percent of total population)	1995-2012	Czech Republic
18	At-risk-of-poverty (percent of elderly population)	1995-2013	Hungary
19	Income quintile share ratio S80/S20	1995-2013	Slovenia
20	GINI coefficient	1995-2013	Slovenia
21	Early leavers from education and training	1992-2013	Croatia
22	Healthy life years at birth - females	1995-2012	Malta
23	Healthy life years at birth - males	1999-2012	Malta
24	Households with broadband access	2003-2013	Finland
25	Regular Internet use	2003-2013	Luxembourg
26	Share of energy from renewable sources	2004-2012	Sweden
27	Urban population exposure to air pollution by particulate matter PM10	1997-2011	Denmark
28	Publications per million inhabitants	1994-2010	Denmark
29	Proportion of seats in national parliaments held by women	2000-2013	Sweden
30	Current account balance in % of GDP	1975-2013	Netherlands

AN ADDITIONAL WAY OF PRESENTATION ACROSS MANY UNITS AND MANY YEARS

Indicator 1. Life expectancy at birth

S-time-matrix: time when specified level of the indicator was achieved (sorted by last available value)

LEVEL	63	64	65	66	67	68	69	70	71	72	73	74	75	76	77	78	79	80	81	82
Spain												1977	1979	1981	1990	1994	1999	2003	2006	**2009**
Italy														1986	1989	1994	1997	2000	2005	**2010**
France														1987	1990	1994	1999	2004	2006	**2010**
Sweden												1968	1976	1981	1986	1992	1995	2002	**2006**	
Luxembourg								1971	1976	1978	1982	1985	1989	1993	1997	2003	2004	2007	**2011**	
Netherlands														1990	1999	2004	2006	**2010**		
Austria									1973	1977	1981	1985	1987	1992	1996	1999	2003	2006	**2011**	
Cyprus																2000	2005	2007	**2009**	
Germany							1962	1971	1976	1979	1983	1987	1992	1996	1999	2004	2007	**2012**		
United Kingdom														1996	2000	2004	2008	**2012**		
Ireland												1987	1991	1997	2001	2003	2005	**2008**		
Malta								1981	1982	1985	1987	1990	1992	1995	2000	2003	2008	**2011**		
Finland												1981	1989	1993	1996	2001	2004	**2009**		
Greece							1964	1969	1973	1978	1985	1992	1999	2002	**2008**					
Portugal	1961	1962	1964	1969	1971	1974	1976	1977	1979	1981	1985	1988	1993	1998	2001	2004	2006	**2010**		
Belgium							1960	1970	1975	1978	1983	1986	1990	1995	2001	2004	**2010**			
EU 28																2003	2007	**2010**		
Slovenia									1983	1985	1988	1994	1996	2000	2004	2006	2008	**2011**		
Denmark													1976	1990	1997	2001	2004	2009	**2011**	
Czech Republic								1971	1984	1991	1993	1996	2000	2005	2007	**2011**				
Croatia												2004	2008	**2011**						
Poland									1992	1995	1998	2001	2005	**2009**						
Estonia					1994	1995	1996	1998	2001	2003	2005	2008	2009	**2010**						
Slovakia									1973	1986	1993	1999	2004	2008	**2011**					
Hungary						1962	1983	1995	1998	2000	2005	2008	**2011**							
Romania							1970	1997	1998	2002	2004	2006	**2010**							
Bulgaria									1962	1998	2002	2007	**2011**							
Latvia										2007	2008	2010	**2012**							
Lithuania								1995	1996	2007	2008	2009	**2012**							
International frontier									1955	1961	1969	1974	1978	1983	1988	1993	1998	2002	2006	**2012**
China					1980	1984	1988	1993	1999	2004	**2009**									

Life expectancy at birth has been increasing in all countries over time. This is easily observed as the years in bold refer to the latest available observation available for each country and they are on the right hand side for all of them. Horizontal lines show how many steps of life expectancy were achieved in a given country. Portugal has experienced even increase from 63 years in 1961 to 80 years in 1980.

There are substantial differences between countries; the largest difference is between 82 years in the three leading countries and 74 years in the four countries with the lowest life expectancy. China is closing fast to reach and possibly surpass the life expectancy in these countries. International frontier represents the average of values of life expectancy for the top 10 performers in the world. Only three of the EU countries are higher than that international benchmark.

1a. S-time-distance for life expectancy at birth
S-time-distance: time lead (-) or time lag (+) from benchmark international frontier

LEVEL	63	64	65	66	67	68	69	70	71	72	73	74	75	76	77	78	79	80	81	82
Spain												2	1	-1	2	1	1	2	0	-3
Italy														4	1	1	-1	-2	-1	-3
France														4	2	1	1	2	0	-2
Sweden												-6	-2	-2	-2	-2	-3	0	0	
Luxembourg									21	17	13	11	11	10	9	10	6	6	4	
Netherlands															2	6	6	4	4	
Austria									18	16	12	10	9	9	8	5	5	4	4	
Cyprus																7	7	5	3	
Germany									17	15	10	9	8	9	8	6	6	5	6	
United Kingdom																8	7	6	7	6
Ireland												12	13	14	13	10	7	6		
Malta									26	22	16	13	11	9	7	7	5	7	4	
Finland													7	11	11	8	7	6	7	
Greece										4	0	-2	-1	2	4	6	4	6		
Portugal									24	21	16	14	15	15	13	10	8	8		
Belgium									15	14	9	9	8	7	7	7	6	7		
EU 28																10	9	8		
Slovenia									28	25	19	20	17	17	16	13	10	9		
Denmark													2	12	14	13	11	11	10	
Czech Republic									30	30	24	22	21	22	19	18				
Croatia													25	25	23					
Poland									37	34	29	26	27	27						
Estonia									46	43	36	33	30	27						
Slovakia									31	32	29	29	30	28						
Hungary									43	40	36	33	32							
Romania									47	44	37	36								
Bulgaria									43	41	38	36								
Latvia									52	47	41	37								
Lithuania									53	48	40	37								
International frontier									0	0	0	0	0	0	0	0	0	0	0	0
China									44	44	40									

Using the novel generic statistical measure S-time-distance (see Annex) it is possible to describe the disparities between different units by the distance in time when the two compared units reached the same level of the indicator. S-time-matrix above shows that life expectancy of about 81 years was reached in the United Kingdom in 2012; this level was reached by the international frontier in 2006, with S-time-distance lead of 6 years or lag of 6 years for the UK. The approach is universal, understandable, and applicable to a wide variety of fields at both the macro and micro levels.

In the EU there are large differences in life expectancy. There is a wealth of information in these tables not discussed here. Four EU countries are among the 10 best countries in the world, 13 countries from Luxembourg to Slovenia are lagging up to 10 years, five at the bottom even more than 30 years.

1b. S-time-step for life expectancy at birth

S-time-step: time needed to achieve next level of the indicator

LEVEL	63	64	65	66	67	68	69	70	71	72	73	74	75	76	77	78	79	80	81	82
Spain													2.4	2.4	8.6	3.8	5.7	4.0	2.5	3.3
Italy															2.8	5.0	3.0	3.3	5.0	4.3
France															3.5	4.0	5.3	4.3	2.4	4.3
Sweden													8.0	4.7	5.3	5.5	3.5	7.0	4.0	
Luxembourg									4.9	1.8	4.4	2.8	3.9	3.9	3.7	6.4	0.8	3.6	3.3	
Netherlands															9.5	4.5	2.5	4.0		
Austria										3.9	4.5	3.5	2.5	4.5	4.0	3.0	4.9	2.4	4.7	
Cyprus																	5.0	2.0	1.8	
Germany									9.3	4.7	3.0	4.0	3.5	5.1	4.4	3.0	4.6	2.9	5.5	
United Kingdom																4.0	4.0	4.3	3.7	
Ireland													4.4	6.0	3.7	1.9	2.4	2.6		
Malta										1.7	2.5	2.5	2.5	2.5	2.5	5.1	3.8	5.0	2.4	
Finland													8.0	4.1	2.9	4.5	3.5	4.5		
Greece											4.7	3.7	4.8	7.5	7.0	7.3	2.7	5.6		
Portugal		0.7	2.2	4.9	2.3	2.4	2.3	0.9	1.7	2.7	3.7	3.3	5.1	4.6	2.5	3.1	2.4	3.8		
Belgium									9.6	5.0	3.4	4.8	3.2	3.3	5.4	5.5	3.5	4.7		
EU 28																	3.2	3.8		
Slovenia										2.2	2.7	6.1	1.6	4.0	4.2	1.9	2.2	2.8		
Denmark														14.0	6.5	4.3	3.4	4.6	2.3	
Czech Republic									12.9	6.7	2.3	2.7	3.5	5.0	2.5	4.0				
Croatia														4.5	2.6					
Poland										3.0	2.8	2.8	4.5	4.2						
Estonia						0.8	0.4	2.7	2.9	2.0	1.8	2.7	1.0	1.3						
Slovakia									12.5	7.5	5.5	5.0	4.8	2.5						
Hungary							20.9	12.0	3.0	2.2	4.8	2.7	3.1							
Romania							26.9	1.5	3.9	2.3	2.2	3.8								
Bulgaria									35.7	3.4	5.5	3.5								
Latvia										0.8	1.8	1.8								
Lithuania								1.0	11.6	1.0	1.0	2.5								
International frontier										5.9	8.4	5.2	4.0	4.3	5.1	5.4	4.9	3.8	4.5	5.6
China						4.2	4.2	5.0	5.6	5.5	4.6									

The three basic constituents of time distance methodology are S-time-matrix, S-time-distance and S-time-step. The values of S-time-step show the number of years needed in the past to reach the next consecutive level of life expectancy. In the row for EU28 it is 3.8 years, i.e. nearly 4 years were needed for increase in 1 year of life expectancy from level of 79 to the level of 80 years. When expressing dynamics in percentage terms this change would be expressed as growth rate of 0.3% per year. Both statistical measures are valid, 3.8 years and/or 0.3% growth rate per year can add information.

Portugal shows the highest dynamics from countries with data from 1960; from the level of 63 years in 1961 to the level of 80 years in 2010. Bulgaria needed over three decades to move from about 70 years in 1962 to about 71 years in 1998. The matrix provides summary of dynamics over all countries.

Indicator 2. Human Development Index

S-time-matrix: time when specified level of the indicator was achieved (sorted by last available value)

LEVEL	0.70	0.71	0.72	0.73	0.74	0.75	0.76	0.77	0.78	0.79	0.80	0.81	0.82	0.83	0.84	0.85	0.86	0.87	0.88	0.89	0.90	0.91	0.92
Netherlands											1980	1983	1985	1987	1990	1992	1994	1996	1998	2000	2005	2007	**2011**
Germany				1980	1982	1983	1985	1986	1988	1990	1991	1993	1994	1996	1997	1999	2000	2002	2003	2005	2008	**2012**	
Ireland					1981	1983	1985	1987	1989	1991	1992	1993	1994	1995	1997	1998	1999	2000	2002	2004	**2006**		
Sweden											1983	1986	1989	1991	1992	1993	1995	1996	1997	1998	2000	**2010**	
Denmark										1980	1984	1988	1991	1993	1995	1996	1998	2000	2002	2004	**2011**		
Belgium								1981	1983	1985	1987	1989	1990	1992	1993	1995	1996	1998	1999	**2007**			
Austria						1981	1983	1985	1987	1989	1991	1993	1995	1996	1998	2001	2003	2005	2007	**2010**			
France				1980	1982	1984	1986	1988	1989	1991	1992	1994	1995	1997	1998	2000	2001	2004	2006	**2010**			
Finland								1981	1984	1987	1990	1992	1994	1997	1999	2001	2002	2003	2005	**2010**			
Slovenia																2001	2003	2004	2006	**2009**			
Spain	1980	1982	1984	1986	1987	1989	1990	1992	1993	1994	1995	1996	1997	1998	1999	2001	2004	2006	**2009**				
Italy					1981	1984	1986	1988	1990	1991	1993	1995	1996	1998	2000	2001	2002	2004	2005	**2010**			
Luxembourg				1981	1982	1984	1986	1987	1989	1991	1992	1994	1995	1997	1998	2000	**2009**						
United Kingdom						1981	1983	1986	1989	1991	1993	1995	1996	1998	2000	2002	2004	**2008**					
Czech Republic															2001	2002	2003	2005	**2009**				
Greece					1981	1983	1985	1987	1990	1992	1995	1997	2000	2001	2002	2003	2004	**2012**					
Cyprus			1981	1982	1984	1985	1987	1989	1990	1994	1997	2001	2006	2007	**2009**								
Malta			1982	1984	1986	1988	1991	1993	1995	1998	2000	2002	2004	2007	**2010**								
Estonia					1990	1992	1994	1996	1997	1999	2000	2002	2003	2004	2005	**2010**							
Slovakia							1992	1995	1998	2001	2003	2004	2006	2007	**2012**								
Hungary		1982	1991	1992	1993	1995	1996	1997	1999	2000	2002	2003	2005	**2011**									
Poland									2001	2003	2006	2008	**2012**										
Lithuania						1993	1998	2000	2002	2003	2004	2005	**2010**										
Portugal	1988	1989	1991	1992	1994	1995	1997	1998	2000	2003	2006	**2008**											
Latvia	1990	1993	1995	1998	2000	2001	2002	2003	2004	2005	2006	**2011**											
Romania		2000	2001	2002	2003	2004	2006	2007	**2008**														
Bulgaria	1989	1994	1999	2001	2003	2004	2006	2008	**2011**														
Very high human dev.											1982	1984	1986	1988	1991	1993	1995	1997	1999	2001	2003	2005	**2010**

The Human Development Index (HDI) published by UNDP is a composite indicator with well documented database and continuous improvements, combining health index, education index, and income index giving a broad vision of the advance of countries in furthering capabilities. EU countries with respect to the HDI were in the very high human development group occupying positions from 4 to 47 in the world ranking, except Romania and Bulgaria occupying positions 56 and 57.

There was a continuous increase in the HDI in all analysed countries as increase in health and education components compensated possible problems in the income index. In non-income HDI the best five EU countries were positioned in the world table Ireland at rank 4, Germany rank 7, Netherlands rank 8, Sweden rank 12, and Slovenia rank 13.

2a. S-time-distance for Human Development Index

S-time-distance: time lead (-) or time lag (+) from benchmark average for very high human development

LEVEL	0.70	0.71	0.72	0.73	0.74	0.75	0.76	0.77	0.78	0.79	0.80	0.81	0.82	0.83	0.84	0.85	0.86	0.87	0.88	0.89	0.90	0.91	0.92
Netherlands											-6	-6	-6	-5	-5	-5	-5	-5	-5	-6	-4		
Germany									5	4	3	3	2	1	1	0	0	-1	-1	-2	-5		
Ireland									6	6	5	4	3	2	1	0	-1	-2	-3	-3	-6		
Sweden											-4	-3	-2	-2	-2	-3	-4	-5	-6	-7	-10		
Denmark										-4	-2	-1	0	0	0	0	0	0	-1	-1	1		
Belgium									1	1	1	0	0	-1	-1	-2	-2	-3	-4	1			
Austria									5	5	4	4	4	4	4	4	5	5	4	4			
France									8	7	6	5	5	4	4	3	3	3	3	4			
Finland									2	3	4	4	4	4	4	4	3	3	2	5			
Slovenia																5	4	3	3	4			
Spain									11	10	9	8	6	6	5	4	5	5	6				
Italy									10	9	9	8	7	7	6	6	5	5	7				
Luxembourg									6	5	4	4	3	3	2	2	1	8					
United Kingdom									7	7	7	6	6	5	5	5	5	7					
Czech Republic														8	8	7	6	8					
Greece									11	11	11	12	10	9	8	7	13						
Cyprus									9	10	11	13	15	15	14								
Malta									14	14	14	13	13	15	15								
Estonia									17	17	15	14	13	12	16								
Slovakia									17	17	16	16	15	14	17								
Hungary									17	16	16	15	14	18									
Poland									19	19	19	19	21										
Lithuania									21	20	19	22											
Portugal									18	19	20	19											
Latvia									22	21	20	23											
Romania									26														
Bulgaria									29														
Very high human dev.									0	0	0	0	0	0	0	0	0	0	0	0	0		

The lead or lag from the benchmark of the average value of the HDI for the very high human development group indicates that four EU countries were ahead of that benchmark, for six further countries from Denmark to Slovenia the time lag was up to five years, for next five countries the lag was below 10 years, for next five between 13 and 18 years, and for six countries between 21 and 29 years.

This ordering also indicates that there were large differences between EU countries in the analysed period of three decades. The largest difference is between Netherlands and Bulgaria, the absolute difference in HDI is 0.139, in percentage terms Bulgaria is 15.1 percent lower than Netherlands, and the time distance was more than 32 years. Similar results are shown also for Romania, for Latvia the corresponding values are 0.107, 11.6 percent, and S-time-distance around 29 years.

2b. S-time-step for Human Development Index

S-time-step: time needed to achieve next level of the indicator

LEVEL	0.7	0.71	0.72	0.73	0.74	0.75	0.76	0.77	0.78	0.79	0.8	0.81	0.82	0.83	0.84	0.85	0.86	0.87	0.88	0.89	0.9	0.91	0.92
Netherlands												2.3	2.3	2.3	2.3	2.1	2.0	2.0	2.0	2.0	5.4	1.7	3.7
Germany						1.5	1.5	1.5	1.5	1.5	1.5	1.5	1.5	1.5	1.5	1.5	1.5	1.5	1.6	1.6	1.6	3.4	3.8
Ireland							2.1	2.1	2.1	2.1	1.4	1.2	1.2	1.2	1.2	1.2	1.2	1.2	1.2	1.8	1.8	1.8	
Sweden												3.2	3.2	1.9	1.3	1.3	1.3	1.3	1.3	1.3	1.3	9.9	
Denmark											3.8	3.8	3.1	1.9	1.9	1.9	1.9	1.9	2.1	2.1	6.1		
Belgium								1.9	1.9	1.9	1.9	1.8	1.5	1.5	1.5	1.5	1.5	1.5	7.3				
Austria					2.0	2.0	2.0	2.0	2.0	2.0	2.0	2.0	2.0	2.0	2.0	2.1	2.6	2.3	1.7	2.3			
France				1.8	1.8	1.8	1.8	1.8	1.6	1.5	1.5	1.5	1.5	1.4	1.5	1.9	2.1	2.2	3.9				
Finland									2.9	2.9	2.9	2.3	2.3	2.3	2.3	1.8	1.3	1.4	1.3	5.3			
Slovenia																	1.5	1.5	1.6	3.7			
Spain		1.7	1.7	1.7	1.7	1.7	1.5	1.1	1.1	1.1	1.1	1.1	1.1	1.1	1.1	1.6	2.8	2.4	3.0				
Italy					2.1	2.1	2.1	2.1	1.7	1.6	1.6	1.6	1.6	1.6	1.5	1.4	1.4	1.5	4.5				
Luxembourg						1.6	1.6	1.6	1.6	1.6	1.6	1.5	1.5	1.5	1.5	1.5	1.5	9.2					
United Kingdom							2.8	2.8	2.8	2.2	1.8	1.8	1.8	1.8	1.8	2.1	2.1	4.0					
Czech Republic																1.3	1.3	1.3	4.3				
Greece						2.2	2.2	2.2	2.2	2.5	2.6	2.6	2.6	1.0	1.0	1.0	1.0	8.2					
Cyprus				1.6	1.6	1.6	1.6	1.6	1.8	3.5	3.5	3.9	4.5	1.8	1.1								
Malta			2.3	2.3	2.3	2.3	2.3	2.3	2.3	2.3	2.0	1.9	3.5	2.3									
Estonia				1.7	1.7	1.7	1.7	1.7	1.5	1.1	1.1	1.1	1.1	5.2									
Slovakia								3.2	3.2	2.5	1.7	1.7	1.5	1.1	5.0								
Hungary			8.8	1.3	1.3	1.3	1.3	1.3	1.3	1.3	1.7	1.7	1.7	6.0									
Poland											2.5	2.5	2.3	3.7									
Lithuania						4.2	2.9	1.1	1.1	1.1	1.1	5.2											
Portugal	1.4	1.4	1.4	1.5	1.5	1.5	1.5	1.4	1.5	3.1	3.6	1.5											
Latvia	4.0	2.6	2.6	2.6	2.2	0.9	0.9	0.9	0.9	0.9	1.2	5.2											
Romania			1.1	1.1	1.1	1.1	1.2	1.2	0.9														
Bulgaria	3.2	4.8	5.9	1.9	1.4	1.4	1.9	1.6	3.4														
Very high human dev.											2.3	2.3	2.3	2.2	2.0	2.0	2.0	2.0	2.1	2.3	2.4	4.2	

The matrix for S-time-step indicates the magnitude of HDI dynamics over the three decades (1980-2012) by the selected levels. At a glance one can see many improvements in the HDI level, though for some countries with missing HDI data (i.e. time series in the UNDP database starting later than in 1980) the progress can be underestimated by the visual impression in the picture. The highest number of increase in the HDI level was in Germany and Spain.

For the average of the very high human development group S-time-step between levels 0.89 and 0.90 was 4.2 years. Again in percentage terms it would be around 0.3% per year. Both measures are valid description of the dynamics of change. For general public it might be even easier to understand that in the current past in HDI about 4.2 years were needed to achieve one step of 0.01 in the HDI.

Indicator 3. GDP per capita in PPS

S-time-matrix: time when specified level of the indicator was achieved (sorted by last available value)

LEVEL	4000	6000	8000	10000	12000	14000	16000	18000	20000	22000	24000	26000	28000	30000	32000	34000	36000	38000	40000	...	66000	68000
Luxembourg																1996	1998	1998	1999		**2011**	2007
Austria									1995	1998	1999	2002	2005	2009	**2011**							
Ireland							1996	1997	1998	1999	2000	2001	2002	2003	**2011**	2008	2007					
Netherlands									1997	1998	1999	2001	2004	2005	**2010**							
Sweden									1997	1999	2000	2003	2005	2010	**2012**							
Denmark									1996	1998	1999	2003	2005	2009	**2012**							
Germany									1997	2000	2003	2005	2009	**2011**								
Belgium									1997	1999	2000	2004	2009	**2011**								
Finland								1995	1997	1999	2000	2003	2005	**2010**								
EU 15									1996	1998	2000	2004	**2009**									
France									1996	1999	2000	2004	**2009**									
United Kingdom									1996	1998	1999	2001	2003	**2008**								
Italy									1995	1998	2000	2005	**2008**									
EU 28								1997	1999	2001	2005	**2010**										
Spain							1996	1998	2000	2002	2004	2006	**2008**									
Cyprus							1997	1999	2002	2004	2006	**2009**										
Malta							1998	2000	2005	**2009**												
Slovenia						1996	1999	2001	2004	2005	**2008**											
Czech Republic						1996	2001	2003	2005	**2011**												
Portugal						1996	1999	2001	**2005**													
Slovakia			1997	2001	2004	2005	2007	**2010**														
Greece						1997	1999	2000	2002	**2011**	2009											
Lithuania		1997	2001	2003	2005	2009	2011	**2012**														
Estonia		1996	1999	2002	2004	2005	2010	**2012**														
Poland			1998	2003	2006	2008	**2011**															
Hungary			1996	2000	2002	2005	**2010**															
Latvia		1998	2002	2004	2006	2010	**2012**															
Croatia			1997	2001	2004	**2006**																
Romania		2002	2005	2007	**2011**																	
Bulgaria	1997	2001	2005	2007	**2012**																	

The step in level of GDP per capita (at purchasing power standard) was set at difference of 2,000 euro to shorten the matrix for presentation. In the current depression only three countries decreased GDP per capita for this amount or more: Greece as expected and Luxembourg from the extraordinarily high value, Ireland for two steps. The time matrix does not convey the message of the setback and damage done by existing world financial system in the current depression.

Smaller level step of 500 or 1,000 Euro could look into the situation in more detail but it could not in one simple table provide also the perception of the great disparities between countries. Values for Austria, Ireland, Netherlands, Sweden, and Denmark are in the range of 32,000, for Romania and Bulgaria in the range of 12,000, a ratio of about 2.7.

Indicator 4. Median income in PPS

S-time-matrix: time when specified level of the indicator was achieved (sorted by last available value)

LEVEL	3000	4000	5000	6000	7000	8000	9000	10000	11000	12000	13000	14000	15000	16000	17000	18000	19000	20000	...	26000	27000
Luxembourg																	1996	1997		2004	**2009**
Austria											1996	1999	2000	2004	2005	2007	2010	**2011**			
Sweden													2006	2007	2008	2008	**2011**				
Finland									1997	2000	2003	2005	2006	2008	2009	2012	**2013**				
Cyprus													2005	2006	2006	2007	**2011**				
Netherlands									1996	1997	1998	2001	2003	2005	2006	2007	**2012**				
Germany										1995	1997	1999	2000	2006	2007	**2011**					
France										1997	1998	2004	2006	2007	2008	**2011**					
Denmark														2006	2007	**2010**					
Belgium										1996	1998	2004	2006	2008	**2011**						
United Kingdom									1996	1999	2000	2001	2003	**2011**	2008						
Ireland						1995	1997	1998	2000	2001	2004	2005	2006	**2009**	2008						
Italy						1995	1998	1999	2002	2004	2006	**2008**									
Malta										2006	2008	**2011**									
Slovenia										2006	2007	**2012**									
Spain					1997	1999	2000	2001	2006	**2010**											
Czech Republic						2006	2007	**2011**													
Greece				1996	1999	2001	**2012**	2011	2011												
Slovakia		2005	2006	2007	2008	2009	**2011**														
Portugal				1998	2000	**2007**															
Poland			2006	2007	2008	**2011**															
Estonia			2005	2006	2007	**2009**															
Hungary				2006	**2011**																
Croatia					**2010**																
Lithuania		2005	2006	**2011**	2009																
Latvia		2005	2006	**2012**	2009																
Bulgaria		2007	**2008**																		
Romania	**2008**																				

Median income shows more declines in the depression. For United Kingdom, Ireland, Lithuania, Latvia the fall was at least of 1,000 euro, for Greece at least 2,000 euro. Also, Portugal did not move by this step beyond the approximate 2007 level, Italy, Bulgaria, Romania did not move for one step beyond the 2008 level, and Estonia not beyond 2009 level. For countries at higher values it is easier to increase by the absolute 1,000 euro step because of their higher starting value but same absolute increase would show lower percentage increase, ceteris paribus.

The perception of the great disparities between countries is confirmed also at the median income levels. Austria at approximate level 20,000, on the one hand, and Romania with 3,000, on the other, show a ratio of about 6.7 – a tremendous gap that can be analysed also between other countries.

Indicator 5. Employment rate (15 to 64 years)

S-time-matrix: time when specified level of the indicator was achieved (sorted by last available value)

LEVEL	51	52	53	54	55	56	57	58	59	60	61	62	63	64	65	66	67	68	69	70	71	72	73	74	75	76	77
Netherlands														1994	1995	1996	1996	1997	1997	1998	1999	1999	2000	2006	**2012**	2009	2009
Sweden																				1998	1999	1999	**2011**	2008	1992		
Germany														1998	2004	2005	2006	2006	2007	2008	2010	**2011**					
Denmark																							2011	2010	2009	2009	2008
Austria															2004	2005	2006	2007	**2011**								
United Kingdom																1994	1996	**2012**	2008								
Finland											1995	1996	1997	1998	1998	1999	2000	2005	**2011**	2008	2008						
Estonia											2010	2010	2010	2011	2011	2011	**2012**	2008	2008								
Czech Republic														2010	**2011**	1998											
Luxembourg									1996	1997	1998	1999	2004	2008	**2011**												
EU 15										1995	1997	1999	2000	2001	2004	**2009**	2008										
Cyprus															**2012**	2012	2011	2011	2009	2008	2007						
EU 28														2004	**2010**	2009											
Slovenia												1996	2003	2004	**2011**	2010	2009	2009									
France									1998	1999	2000	2002	**2009**														
Latvia						2000	2001	2010	2011	2012	**2012**	2009	2008	2008	2008	2008											
Lithuania								2010	2011	2011	2011	**2012**	2008	2008													
Belgium							1995	1997	1998	1999	2004	2006	**2010**														
Portugal													**2012**	2012	2011	2010	2009	2009	2008	2001							
Poland		2004	2005	2006	2006	2007	2007	2007	**2010**																		
Slovakia							2004	2005	**2010**	2009	2009	2008															
Romania								2005	**2012**	2002	2001	2001	2000	1998	1997												
Malta				2006	2009	2010	2011	2011	**2012**																		
Bulgaria	2002	2003	2003	2004	2005	2005	2005	2006	**2011**	2010	2010	2009	2009	2008													
Ireland		1993	1994	1995	1996	1996	1997	1997	**2011**	2010	2009	2009	2009	2009	2008	2008	2008	2007									
Hungary			1997	1998	1999	2011	**2012**																				
Italy	1995	1998	1999	2000	2001	2003	**2010**	2009																			
Spain	1998	1998	1999	1999	1999	**2012**	2011	2011	2010	2009	2009	2009	2008	2008	2007												
Greece		**2012**	2012	2011	2011	2011	2011	2010	2010	2010	2009																
Croatia	**2012**	2011	2011	2010	2010	2009	2009																				

Employment rates show vast differences among EU countries, ranging in 2012 between 75 percent in Netherlands to 51 percent in Croatia. According to these figures from Eurostat obviously other forms of labour utilisation must be important and employment policies must deal with such vast differences.

Only eight countries did not experience a drop in the employment rate for the whole one point or more. Both for the EU28 and EU15 averages there was a fall in the employment rate indicating that these eight countries were not able to compensate the decrease in other 20 EU countries during the recent crisis. In Netherlands, Czech Republic, Slovenia, and Italy the fall was about one point in the rate, the highest hit were Ireland (10), Greece and Spain (9), Portugal (7), Cyprus and Croatia (6). It is the fall in the employment rate that shows the magnitude of the blow of the financial crisis in developed world to the EU (and USA); the fall in the GDP per capita undervalues the severity of the current depression.

Indicator 6. Activity rate (15 to 64 years)

S-time-matrix: time when specified level of the indicator was achieved (sorted by last available value)

LEVEL	58	59	60	61	62	63	64	65	66	67	68	69	70	71	72	73	74	75	76	77	78	79	80	81	82
Sweden																				1999	2005	2010	**2011**		
Netherlands											1993	1994	1996	1996	1997	1998	1999	2000	2001	2005	2007	**2012**			
Denmark																						**2011**	2009	1993	1992
Germany														1999	2003	2004	2005	2006	2008	**2011**					
United Kingdom																	**2012**								
Austria														2001	2005	2005	2006	**2008**							
Finland															1994	1998	1999	**2011**	2008						
Estonia													2004	2005	2006	2007	**2010**								
Latvia												2001	2003	2005	2006	2006	2011	**2012**							
Spain		1995	1995	1996	1997	1998	1999	2001	2002	2003	2003	2004	2005	2006	2007	2009	**2012**								
Portugal												1995	1997	1999	2001	2004	**2012**								
Cyprus														2001	2002	2003	**2009**								
EU 15												1997	1999	2003	2005	2007	**2012**								
Lithuania												2007	2008	2010	**2011**	1999									
EU 28												2003	2006	**2011**											
Czech Republic															2009	**2011**	1999								
France												1996	2002	2008	**2012**										
Slovenia											1997	2003	2004	2004	**2010**										
Luxembourg			1996	1998	1999	2000	2003	2004	2008	2011	**2012**														
Slovakia														2011	2003										
Ireland			1993	1995	1996	1997	1998	1998	1999	2000	2003	**2010**	2009	2008											
Greece		1993	1994	1996	1997	1998	2002	2003	2004	2007	**2010**														
Bulgaria				2003	2005	2005	2006	2006	2011	**2012**															
Belgium				1993	1995	1997	1998	2003	2004	**2011**															
Poland						2008	2010	**2011**																	
Hungary	1997	1998	2002	2005	2010	2011	**2012**																		
Romania						2009	**2012**	2002	2001	2001	2000	1998													
Italy	1996	1998	2000	2002	2003	**2012**																			
Malta	2007	2009	2010	2011	2011	**2012**																			
Croatia				**2011**	2009	2008																			

Activity rates differ less than employment rates but there are still large differences in level as well as in the dynamic of change in time. Netherlands, Spain, Ireland and Greece increased activity rate over many levels. For the last three of them most of the increase in the activity rate was taking place before the crisis, which was the general characteristic also for most of other countries.

During the current depression for seven countries activity rate decreased, for one level in Finland, Lithuania, Czech Republic, Slovakia, for two levels in Ireland and Croatia, and for three levels in Denmark.

Disparities remain high also for activity rates, in the range of approximate 80 percent for Sweden and 61 percent for Croatia, with a ratio of 1.31.

Indicator 7. Share of gross fixed investment in GDP

S-time-matrix: time when specified level of the indicator was achieved (sorted by last available value)

LEVEL	10	11	12	13	14	15	16	17	18	19	20	21	22	23	24	25	26	27	28	29	30	31	32	33	34	35
Estonia									1995	1996	1996	1996	2010	2010	2011	2011	2011	**2012**	2008	2008	2008	2008	2008	2008	2007	
Romania									1996	2000	2002	2003	2004	2005	2005	2005	2006	**2013**	2012	2009	2009	2008	2008	2008	2008	1995
Czech Republic											1993	1994	**2012**	2011	2009	2008	1996									
Bulgaria	1997	1998	1998	1999	1999	2000	2000	2001	2001	2002	2003	2004	**2013**	2010	2010	2010	2010	2009	2009	2009	2009	2008	2008			
Croatia						1995	1995	1996	1996	1996	2001	2002	2002	**2011**	2010	2010	2009	2009	2009	2008						
Lithuania						1995	1996	1996	1997	2010	2012	**2013**	2009	2008	2008	2008	2008	2008	2007							
Luxembourg									1995	1997	2010	2011	**2012**	2008												
Austria									**2010**	2008	2005	2001	1997	1977												
Poland						1995	1996	2005	2006	2006	**2012**	2009														
Latvia			1995	1996	1996	1997	1997	1997	2010	2010	2011	**2013**	2012	2009	2009	2008	2008	2008	2008	2008	2008	2007	2007			
Slovakia											2012	2012	2011	2011	2008	2007	2001	1999	1999	1999	1998	1998	1998			
Spain									1984	1985	**2012**	2011	2010	2009	2009	2009	2008	2008	2008	2007						
Belgium											2003	**2011**	2008													
Finland								1995	1995	**2013**	2008	1991	1991	1991	1990	1990	1989	1976	1975							
Sweden						1994	1995	2004	2010	**2013**	2008	1967														
Hungary										**2012**	2010	2010	2009	2009												
Denmark			1981	1983	1984	1994	1995	1996	**2011**	2009	2008	2007														
France						1954	1956	1997	1999	**2011**	2008	1975	1973													
Slovenia						1992	1993	1994	**2013**	2011	2010	2010	2010	2009	2009	2009	2009	2008	2008	2008						
Germany									**2008**	2001	1992															
Italy									**2012**	2010	2008	2007														
Netherlands							**2013**	2009	2009	2008	2000	1972	1972	1971												
Portugal							**2012**	2012	2011	2011	2010	2009	2008	2005	2003	2002	2001									
United Kingdom				1981	1984	**2009**	2008	2008																		
Ireland						**2011**	2010	2010	2010	2009	2009	2009	2009	2009	2008	2008	2008	2008	2007							
Greece						**2013**	2012	2011	2011	2011	2010	2010	2009	2009	2008	2008	2008	2007	2007							
Cyprus						**2013**	2012	2012	2012	2011	2011	2010	2010	2009	2008											
Malta				**2012**	2011	2011	2011	2010	2010	2008	2007	2007	2005													
EU 28									**2012**	2009	2008	2007														
EU 15									**2011**	2009	2008															
United States			1976	1993	1994	1994	1995	1995	1996	1998	**2011**	2008	2008	2007												
Japan											**2013**	2008	2007	2003	2001	2000	1998	1997	1993	1992	1991					

Share of gross fixed investment in GDP indicates the relative effort to increase the fixed capital as one of the factors of production and together with the productivity of capital determines the medium/long-term rate of growth of GDP. The S-time-matrix for this share provides really at a glance the disastrous effects of the world financial system in the current depression on the GDP growth rates. In all 28 EU countries without exception the investment share decreased, for EU15 average and the USA for 3 steps. Ireland and Greece had the largest drops for even 13 steps (from share of 26 percent in 2007 to 13 percent in 2013), followed by Latvia and Slovenia with 11 steps, Bulgaria 10, Spain and Cyprus 9, Malta 8, Estonia, Lithuania, and Romania 7, Croatia 6, Slovakia 5, Hungary 4, etc. Stories in this time matrix demonstrate in excellent way very clearly the disaster in the current depression.

Indicator 8. R&D expenditure (GERD), percent of GDP

S-time-matrix: time when specified level of the indicator was achieved (sorted by last available value)

LEVEL	0.3	0.5	0.7	0.9	1.1	1.3	1.5	1.7	1.9	2.1	2.3	2.5	2.7	2.9	3.1	3.3	3.5	3.7	3.9	4.1
Finland						1983	1985	1987	1990	1992	1995	1996	1997	1998	1999	2000	2007	**2011**	2010	
Sweden										1982	1984	1991	1992	1993	1995	**2010**	2008	2002	2001	
Denmark			1982	1986	1989	1993	1997	1998	2000	2006	2007	2008	**2009**							
Germany										1998	2004	2008	**2011**							
Austria					1981	1988	1994	1997	1999	2002	2004	2007	**2009**							
Slovenia						2003	2007	2008	2009	2010	2011	2011	**2012**							
France									1981	**2008**	1994									
Belgium								1995	2007	**2010**										
Estonia		2001	2005	2007	2008	2009	2010	2010	2011	**2011**										
Netherlands									2010	**2012**										
EU 15									2005	**2010**										
EU 28										**2008**										
Czech Republic					1999	2008	2010	**2011**												
Ireland						2002	2007	2008	**2012**											
United Kingdom									2005	1995	1989	1982								
Luxembourg									**2009**											
Portugal			1999	2006	2007	2007	**2012**													
Hungary			1999	2004	2009	**2012**														
Spain		1984	1988	2000	2005	**2012**														
Italy					**2005**															
Lithuania			1999	2003	**2012**															
Poland				2009	**2012**															
Malta	2003	2004	**2011**																	
Slovakia		2009	**2011**	1998	1994	1993														
Croatia				**2008**																
Greece		**1996**																		
Latvia		2009	**2011**																	
Bulgaria		**2009**	1995	1994	1993	1993	1992	1991	1991	1990	1990									
Cyprus	2002	**2011**																		
Romania		**2011**	1996																	

The share of GDP devoted to R&D expenditures differs greatly among EU countries. The values in Finland and Sweden were 5 times higher than in seven countries (Malta, Slovakia, Greece, Latvia, Bulgaria, Cyprus, and Romania). The average for the EU is below 2 percent, with 10 countries above the average and 18 countries below that. Of the countries that joined in 2004 or later only Slovenia with 2.7 percent and Estonia with about 2.3 percent belong to the above the average group.

There are several factors behind the differences, among them the structure of the economy and development targets. In general the trend towards higher shares has been observed in the analysed period, with exception of United Kingdom, Slovakia, and Bulgaria that were enjoying higher values in the previous century. The fact that the EU average is below 2 percent means that EU is considerably below USA and Japan, much below the desired 3 percent aimed at already in the Lisbon Strategy.

Indicator 9. Summary Innovation Index

S-time-matrix: time when specified level of the indicator was achieved (sorted by last available value)

LEVEL	0.20	0.24	0.28	0.32	0.36	0.40	0.44	0.48	0.52	0.56	0.60	0.64	0.68	0.72
Sweden														2008
Germany													2008	2012
Denmark													2010	
Finland													2011	
Netherlands											2011	2012		
Luxembourg											2011			
Belgium											2009			
United Kingdom											2009			
Austria											2012			
Ireland										2010				
France									2008	2011				
EU 27									2009					
Slovenia								2009						
Cyprus								2010						
Estonia							2009	2011						
Italy						2008	2012							
Spain						2012								
Portugal						2009								
Czech Republic						2010								
Greece					2010									
Slovakia				2012										
Hungary				2010										
Malta				2010										
Lithuania			2012											
Poland			2011											
Latvia	2009													
Romania		2011												
Bulgaria	2012													

This time matrix is an excellent example of how time matrices can really at a glance provide the perception of vast differences in Summary Innovation Index as a composite indicator from Innovation Union Scoreboard. It is true that the time series of the composite indicator are very short, 2008-2012. Yet there are only five countries, Germany, Netherlands, France, Estonia and Italy that were able increase the one step in the summary innovation index in that period – the step was to increase it by 0.04.

Such step in the matrix was chosen so that such a large range of values from 0.2 for Latvia and Bulgaria to 0.72 in Sweden and Germany could be presented in one matrix. Of course, one could make the steps smaller to see the situation in countries in more detail (and use the Time Matrix Calculator in the Annex). Yet this compressed S-time-matrix delivers immediately visually with time and with levels the message of the vast differences and ordering of individual countries.

Indicator 10. Tertiary attainment for age group 15-64

S-time-matrix: time when specified level of the indicator was achieved (sorted by last available value)

LEVEL	12	13	14	15	16	17	18	19	20	21	22	23	24	25	26	27	28	29	30	31	32	33	34	35	36
Ireland									2000	2001	2002	2003	2003	2004	2005	2006	2006	2007	2008	2009	2009	2011	2012	2012	**2013**
United Kingdom															2004	2005	2006	2008	2009	2010	2010	2011	2012	**2012**	
Cyprus											2001	2001	2002	2005	2006	2006	2007	2007	2009	2010	2011	2011	**2012**		
Luxembourg		2003	2003	2003	2003	2004	2004	2004	2004	2006	2007	2007	2008	2008	2008	2009	2009	2009	2009	2011	2011	2012	2012	**2013**	
Finland																2002	2004	2006	2007	2009	2010	**2012**			
Estonia													2002	2004	2005	2008	2009	2010	2011	2012	**2013**				
Belgium												2000	2002	2003	2005	2007	2009	2009	**2012**						
Sweden													2002	2003	2004	2006	2008	2010	2011	2012	**2013**				
Spain											2001	2003	2004	2005	2006	2009	2010	2011	**2012**						
Lithuania								2002	2003	2004	2005	2006	2007	2008	2009	2010	2011	**2012**							
Netherlands										2001	2002	2003	2003	2004	2005	2007	2011	**2013**							
Denmark												2000	2000	2001	2002	2007	2009	2011	**2013**						
France									2000	2001	2003	2004	2006	2008	2009	2011	**2012**								
Latvia				2004	2005	2006	2007	2008	2008	2009	2010	2011	2012	2012	**2013**										
EU 15										2001	2003	2004	2007	2008	2010	2011	**2012**								
EU 28						2003	2004	2006	2008	2009	2010	2011	**2013**												
Germany									2002	2003	2008	2009	2010	2011	**2013**										
Slovenia	2002	2002	2003	2003	2004	2005	2006	2008	2010	2011	2011	2012	**2013**												
Greece		2002	2003	2004	2005	2007	2009	2010	2011	2012	**2013**														
Poland	2003	2004	2005	2006	2007	2008	2009	2010	2011	2012	**2012**														
Bulgaria				2000	2001	2006	2008	2011	2012	**2013**															
Hungary	2002	2003	2004	2006	2008	2009	2011	**2012**																	
Czech Republic	2008	2009	2010	2010	2011	2012	**2013**																		
Austria				2008	2009	**2012**																			
Portugal	2007	2009	2010	2011	2011	**2012**																			
Slovakia	2007	2009	2009	2010	2011	**2012**																			
Malta	2008	2010	2011	2012	**2013**																				
Croatia			2008	2009	**2012**																				
Italy	2007	2010	**2012**																						
Romania	2010	**2011**																							

Tertiary attainment for the age group 15-64 years is constantly increasing with entries of the younger population with higher attainment rates. Dynamics is high but disparities remain large. Nine countries surpassed level of 30 percent of tertiary attainment but even the best EU countries are below the values attainted e.g. in Canada, Israel, Japan, and in the USA.

According to Eurostat data there were 9 countries with levels below 20 percent of tertiary attainment with some surprising cases (Hungary, Czech Republic, Austria, Portugal, Slovakia, Malta, Croatia, Italy, and Romania).

There is not much difference between the average values for EU15 and EU28, with about 26 percent and 25 percent in 2011, respectively.

Indicator 11. Proportion of population aged 65 years and more (percent)

S-time-matrix: time when specified level of the indicator was achieved (sorted by last available value)

LEVEL	6	7	8	9	10	11	12	13	14	15	16	17	18	19	20	21
Italy					1966	1971	1975	1985	1988	1991	1994	1996	2000	2003	2007	2013
Germany							1963	1967	1972	1993	1999	2002	2004	2006	2008	
Greece			1963	1969	1970	1971	1975	1979	1992	1995	1998	2001	2004	2010	2013	
Portugal			1962	1969	1975	1979	1986	1990	1992	1996	2000	2004	2009	2012		
Bulgaria			1964	1968	1972	1976	1988	1990	1993	1995	1999	2003	2009	2013		
Sweden							1962	1967	1972	1975	1979	1985	2010	2013		
Finland			1966	1970	1974	1977	1981	1989	1995	2001	2006	2010	2012			
Latvia							1991	1994	1997	2001	2004	2006	2010			
EU 28											2002	2007	2012			
Lithuania					1970	1991	1994	1998	2001	2003	2005	2008	2012			
Austria								1965	1970	1994	2005	2008	2013			
Croatia												2004	2013			
Estonia							1992	1994	1997	2000	2004	2006	2013			
Denmark						1963	1969	1974	1978	2005	2009	2011				
France							1965	1986	1991	1995	2000	2011				
Spain				1967	1974	1981	1985	1989	1992	1995	1998	2011				
Belgium							1961	1968	1986	1991	1996	2003				
Hungary				1961	1964	1968	1973	1989	1995	2000	2007	2012				
Malta			1982	1985	1988	1995	1999	2004	2008	2010	2011	2013				
United Kingdom							1963	1971	1976	1985	2009	2013				
Slovenia							1992	1995	1997	2001	2004	2007	2013			
Czech Republic					1963	1967	1987	1994	2004	2009	2012					
Netherlands				1961	1969	1977	1985	1993	2005	2009	2012					
Romania				1973	1989	1992	1996	1999	2002	2005	2010					
Poland	1961	1966	1969	1973	1990	1995	2000	2004	2013							
Luxembourg							1962	1968	1975	2013						
Cyprus			1963	1967	1971	1976	1996	2005	2013							
Slovakia			1961	1966	1970	1989	1997	2007	2013							
Ireland						2009	2012									

On the demographic side it is interesting to look at the aging of the population in the last five decades. Italy, Germany, and Greece already surpassed the 20 percent share of the population aged 65 years or more. The next group is formed by Portugal, Bulgaria, and Sweden; next seven countries reached the share of 17 percent, eight countries 16 percent, and three countries 15 percent share. The lowest value was reached in five countries with below 15 percent, with Ireland at 12 percent. The world average at less than 10 percent is much lower than that for the EU.

The trend towards higher share in the total population is very clear. Time distance estimates indicate that the differences within EU are large and changing very slowly. For instance, time distance between Ireland and Italy at level 12 percent was 37 years (2012-1975).

Indicator 12. Old age dependency ratio, projections 2013-2080
S-time-matrix: time when specified level of the indicator was achieved

LEVEL	20	22	24	26	28	30	32	34	36	38	40	42	44	46	48	50	52	54	56	58	60	62	64	66	68
Slovakia	2015	2017	2020	2022	2024	2027	2029	2032	2035	2037	2040	2041	2043	2044	2046	2047	2048	2050	2052	2053	2055	2057	2058	2070	**2077**
Portugal						2014	2017	2020	2022	2024	2026	2029	2031	2032	2034	2036	2038	2039	2041	2043	2045	2048	2061	2070	**2079**
Spain			2016	2019	2022	2024	2026	2028	2030	2032	2033	2035	**2078**	2065	2062	2060	2057	2055	2053	2051					
Greece						2015	2019	2023	2025	2028	2031	2032	2034	2036	2037	2039	2041	2043	**2066**	2062	2056				
Poland		2015	2017	2019	2021	2024	2026	2028	2031	2036	2040	2042	2043	2045	2047	2048	2050	2052	2055	2057	**2065**				
Germany						2014	2017	2020	2022	2024	2026	2027	2029	2031	2034	2036	2038	2043	**2054**						
Bulgaria					2015	2018	2021	2025	2028	2032	2035	2038	2041	2043	2045	2048	**2068**	2065	2061						
Italy							2017	2022	2025	2029	2031	2034	2036	2038	2040	2047	2071	**2078**							
Estonia				2014	2017	2019	2022	2025	2028	2031	2034	2038	2041	2045	**2077**	2064	2061								
Croatia				2014	2017	2020	2023	2026	2029	2032	2036	2041	2044	2048	2053	2059	**2075**								
Austria				2016	2021	2023	2026	2028	2031	2034	2037	2040	2047	2054	2059	2068	**2079**								
Hungary				2014	2017	2019	2024	2029	2033	2037	2040	2043	2046	2048	2051	2055	**2059**								
Slovenia				2014	2016	2018	2020	2023	2025	2027	2029	2032	2035	2038	2041	**2066**	2062								
Netherlands				2014	2016	2019	2021	2023	2026	2028	2030	2033	2036	2038	2061	2068	**2078**								
Czech Republic				2014	2017	2019	2022	2027	2032	2036	2040	2042	2045	**2072**	2065	2061									
Romania			2013	2016	2019	2024	2028	2032	2034	2036	2038	2041	2044	2047	2049	**2070**									
EU 28						2014	2017	2020	2023	2026	2029	2031	2034	2037	2040	2046	**2074**								
Malta				2014	2016	2018	2019	2022	2024	2027	2029	2043	2048	2052	2055	**2074**									
Finland						2014	2016	2018	2020	2024	2028	2050	2057	2065	**2073**										
Cyprus	2015	2017	2020	2023	2025	2028	2031	2035	2039	2043	2046	2049	**2067**	2062											
Denmark						2014	2017	2021	2025	2029	2034	2053	2061	2067	**2075**										
France						2014	2016	2019	2022	2025	2028	2032	2036	2068	**2078**										
Ireland	2015	2018	2021	2024	2027	2030	2032	2074	**2078**	2058	2055	2053	2051												
Belgium						2016	2021	2025	2029	2036	2050	2061	2070	**2077**											
United Kingdom							2017	2021	2025	2028	2033	2037	2046	2057	**2077**										
Sweden							2013	2018	2024	2033	2051	2056	2070	**2078**											
Luxembourg			2021	2026	2031	2037	2043	2051	2056	2061	2065	2069	2075	**2080**											

Legend	2013-2030	2031-2050	2051-2080

Eurostat prepared projections for the old age dependency ratio for the period 2013-2080. This time matrix is an example how projections over the period of 67 years and 28 countries (with some interpolations encompassing potential 1876 entries) can be presented in a compressed single one page table. The colours distinguish the three sub-periods: 2013-2030, 2031-2050, and 2051-2080.

Looking by sub-periods it is seen that by 2030 Germany will be the country with the highest old age dependency ratio reaching ratio of 46 by about 2029. Yet, by 2080 Germany will not be the country with the highest ratio, in that decade Slovakia and Portugal would have the highest ratio of about 68.

By 2030 behind Germany Portugal will follow, other countries with the highest values will be the group of Finland, Greece, Malta, Slovenia, Italy, and Netherlands. Slovakia, which is projected by 2030 to be in a group with much smaller value of the ratio, is expected to increase the ratio especially after 2050. The average for EU28 is expected to grow fast by 2030, but not much beyond 2050.

12a. S-time-distance for old age dependency ratio, projections 2013-2080

S-time-distance: time lead (-) or time lag (+) from benchmark Germany

LEVEL	20	22	24	26	28	30	32	34	36	38	40	42	44	46	48	50	52	54	56	58	60	62	64	66	68
Slovakia							15	15	14	15	16	16	15	15	14	13	13	12	9	0					
Portugal							3	2	2	2	3	3	3	3	3	2	2	1	-1	-10					
Spain							8	7	6	6	7	6	6	5	47	32	26	21	15	1					
Greece							1	2	2	3	4	5	5	5	4	4	3	3	0	13					
Poland							12	11	11	14	16	16	16	16	15	15	14	14	12	3					
Germany							0	0	0	0	0	0	0	0	0	0	0	0	0	0					
Bulgaria							4	4	4	6	8	9	11	12	12	12	12	30	22	8					
Italy								0	2	3	5	6	6	7	7	7	11	33	35						
Estonia							5	5	5	6	7	9	10	12	13	43	28	23							
Croatia							6	6	6	7	8	11	13	15	17	19	24	37							
Austria							9	9	8	9	10	11	12	18	22	25	32	41							
Hungary							10	12	13	15	16	17	18	19	20	22	23								
Slovenia							6	5	5	5	6	6	8	9	10	32	26								
Netherlands							7	6	5	6	6	7	8	9	30	35	43								
Czech Republic							8	10	11	14	16	17	17	43	34	27									
Romania							14	14	14	14	15	15	16	17	18	36									
EU 28							6	6	6	7	8	9	10	11	15	40									
Malta							5	4	4	5	6	18	21	23	24	40									
Finland							2	1	0	2	4	25	30	36	42										
Cyprus							16	18	19	21	22	24	40	32											
Denmark							7	8	9	12	29	36	40	45											
France							5	5	5	6	8	10	41	49											
Ireland							18	56	58	36	32	28	23												
Belgium							11	12	15	28	37	45	49												
United Kingdom							11	11	13	15	22	31	49												
Sweden							4	7	13	29	33	45	51												
Luxembourg							37	39	41	43	46	49	52												

In the matrix 12a the possible magnitude of time distance lead and lag against the benchmark Germany are calculated. There are several interpolations, both in the values for each decade as presented in projections itself, as well as interpolations by the years in the time matrix calculation. Therefore, one should not form very precise statements from the values in the table.

Portugal and Greece have very small time distance delays behind Germany in the earlier years, there are very many countries that are following Germany to about value of the ratio at 40 with reasonably small time lag.

There are several countries at the bottom of the table which seem to be reaching and surpassing this level in the period after 2050, notably Denmark, Ireland, Belgium, Sweden, and Luxemburg, very close to this countries are United Kingdom and France. This group of countries are those which will by 2080 display the lowest values for old age dependency ratio in the EU.

Indicator 13. Population growth rates (percent)

S-time-matrix: time when specified level of the indicator was achieved (sorted by last available value)

LEVEL	-4.4	-4	-3.6	-3.2	-2.8	-2.4	-2	-1.6	-1.2	-0.8	-0.4	0	0.4	0.8	1.2	1.6	2	2.4	2.8	3.2	3.6	4	4.4	4.8
Luxembourg												1983	1986	1989	2003	2008	2011	**2013**						
Malta										1984	1984	1984	2011	**2013**	2002	2002	2001	2001	2001	1983	1983			
Sweden													2005	**2011**										
United Kingdom												1983	2002	**2011**										
Belgium												1985	2004	**2012**	2011									
Austria												1985	**2013**	1994										
Italy												1996	**2013**	1966										
Finland											1970	1971	**2007**											
Cyprus									1976	1977	1977	1977	1983	**2013**	2013	2012	2012	2012						
France													**1999**	1974	1964	1964	1963	1963						
Denmark												1985	**2012**	1971										
Netherlands													**2012**	1981	1971									
Germany											1977	**2011**	1994	1993										
EU 28													**2008**											
Ireland											1989	1990	**2011**	2010	2009	2009	2009	2008	2008					
Slovenia												2008	**2011**	2010	1988	1987	1987							
Slovakia												**2005**	1994	1981	1962	1962	1962	1962	1962	1961	1961	1961	1961	1961
Czech Republic										1971	2001	2004	**2010**	2009										
Poland											2000	2001	**2013**	2012	2011	1965								
Spain												**2013**	2011	2010	2009	2009								
Hungary							1990	1990	1990	1991	**2012**	1992	1978											
Croatia	2001	2001	2001	2001	2001	2001	2002	2002	2002	2002	2002	**2007**	1995	1995	1994	1994								
Romania						2002	2008	2009	2009	2010	**2013**	1991	1990	1979	1977									
Estonia				1993	1994	1995	1996	1997	1999	**2008**	2001	2001	2000	2000										
Portugal									1970	1971	**2012**	2011	2003	1982	1977	1977	1977	1977	1977	1976	1976	1976	1976	1976
Greece												**2013**	2010	2000	1995	1992	1979							
Bulgaria						2002	2002	2002	2007	2008	**2008**	1995	1989	1981	1969									
Latvia							2011	2012	**2013**	2008	1991	1990	1990	1989	1965	1961								
Lithuania					2011	2011	2012	2012	**2013**	2003	1993	1992	1990	1990	1972	1962								

Looking at the yearly rates of growth of population there was in the past great variation between the countries. Negative growth rate was exceptional in Croatia due to the war circumstances. In the most recent years (visually noted by the bold figures) with three exceptions all EU countries are in the range from – 0.8 to +0.8 percent growth rate, i.e. in a small range.

The only high increase is in Luxembourg (2.4%), on the negative side Latvia and Lithuania (-1.2 %). There are eight countries with negative rates and 16 countries with positive population growth rates; for EU28 the average growth rate is positive, but at 0.4% not indicating a very large magnitude of immigration effect.

Indicator 14. Persons killed in road accidents per million inhabitants

S-time-matrix: time when specified level of the indicator was achieved (sorted by last available value)

LEVEL	240	230	220	210	200	190	180	170	160	150	140	130	120	110	100	90	80	70	60	50	40	30
United Kingdom																			2003	2007	2009	**2011**
Sweden																			2003	2007	2009	**2010**
Denmark																2000	2003	2008	2009	2010	2011	**2012**
Malta																					2005	**2009**
Netherlands																			2003	2004	**2009**	
Spain											2001	2002	2004	2004	2005	2006	2007	2008	2009	**2010**		
Ireland													2000	2002	2006	2007	2008	2008	**2009**			
Finland															2002	2007	2008	**2012**				
Germany																2000	2003	2004	2007	**2009**		
France												2000	2002	2002	2003	2003	2004	2006	2008	**2012**		
Cyprus								2004	2005	2005	2006	2007	2008	2008	2009	2011	2012	**2012**				
Hungary											2002	2003	2007	2008	2008	2009	2009	**2010**				
Austria												1999	2001	2004	2005	2006	2008	**2010**				
Luxembourg							2000	2001	2001	2002	2002	2003	2004	2005	2009	2010	**2010**					
Portugal						1999	2000	2001	2002	2003	2003	2004	2005	2005	2006	2007	2011	**2012**				
Slovenia											2000	2007	2007	2008	2008	2008	2009	2009	**2010**			
Slovakia														2007	2008	2008	2009	2009	**2010**			
Italy												2002	2004	2005	2007	2008	**2010**					
Czech Republic											2003	2005	2005	2008	2008	2009	**2010**					
Estonia									2002	2006	2007	2007	2008	2008	2008	2008	**2009**					
Belgium											2001	2002	2003	2004	2007	2008	**2010**					
Latvia	2002	2003	2004	2005	2005	2005	2007	2007	2008	2008	2008	2009	2009	2010	2010	**2011**						
Croatia											2008	2009	2009	2009	2010	**2010**						
Poland									2000	2003	2008	2009	2009	2010	**2012**							
Romania												2009	2009	2010	2010	**2011**						
Greece								2000	2000	2001	2002	2005	2008	2009	2010	**2010**						
Bulgaria														**2007**								
United States							1990	1991	1991	2000	2006	2007	2008	**2009**								
Korea		1999	2000	2000	2000	2001	2001	2001	2002	2003	2004	2006	**2009**									

Persons killed in road accidents per million inhabitants are showing continuous improvement but also very large differences among countries in the EU and two comparators USA and Korea. Except for Bulgaria and Greece all EU countries show less fatal road accidents than the USA and Korea. These are the countries which in the trend towards decreasing fatalities did not pass the 100 mark. The ranking might change if the indicator would also consider millions of kilometres travelled in the country.

The best EU countries have already fallen below the 30 persons killed per 1,000,000 inhabitants: United Kingdom, Sweden, and Denmark. In the world, broadly speaking 80-90 people per 1,000,000 inhabitants more are killed on roads in USA and Korea than in the best EU countries. Similarly, 100 more deaths are shown for Bulgaria, 80 for Greece, 70 for Croatia, Poland, and Romania, etc. Germany, Ireland, Spain, and Finland are in terms of time distance lag 2 to 5 years behind the general trend of improvement in the leaders United Kingdom and Sweden.

Indicator 15. Death due to homicide, standardised death rate by 100 000 inhabit.

S-time-matrix: time when specified level of the indicator was achieved (sorted by last available value)

LEVEL	16	15	14	13	12	11	10	9	8	7	6.5	6	5.5	5	4.5	4	3.5	3	2.5	2	1.5	1	0.5
United Kingdom																						1994	2004
Cyprus																				2009	2009	2010	2010
Slovenia																			1997	1997	2004	2007	2010
Austria																						2001	
France																						1997	
Germany																						1997	2009
EU 15																						2000	
Italy																					1994	2005	
Spain																						2005	
Czech Republic																				1995	2000	2007	
Denmark																						2005	
Ireland																						2007	2004
EU 28																						2008	
Netherlands																						2005	
Poland																		1996	1999	2001	2006	2010	
Sweden																						2008	
Malta																				2001	2002	2010	2005
Belgium																			1999	2001	2007		
Portugal																					2006	2009	
Slovakia																			2000	2003	2006		
Croatia																					2009		
Greece																					1998	2007	
Hungary																		1997	1999	2002	2008	2010	
Bulgaria														1996	1997	1998	2000	2002	2005	2009			
Finland																	1996	2002	2009				
Luxembourg																				2010	2009	2009	2004
Romania																2003	2004	2005	2009				
Estonia	2000	2001	2001	2002	2002	2003	2003	2005	2006	2007	2008	2009	2009	2010									
Lithuania			1994	1995	1995	1996	2003	2005	2006	2009	2009	2009											
Latvia	1997	1998	1998	2000	2002	2003	2006	2007	2008	2009													

Time matrix for indicator 15 is another proof of the old saying that picture says more than thousand words. While Estonia, Lithuania, and Latvia have been considerably decreasing the death rate due to homicide, their current values are still very much higher than in other EU countries. This death rate in the best three countries (United Kingdom, Cyprus, and Slovenia) is 10 times lower than that in Estonia; 0.5 per 100,000 inhabitants against 5 in Estonia. The average values for EU15 and EU28 are around 1, i.e. 5 times lower than in Estonia, and even more times lower than in Lithuania and Latvia.

Luxembourg and Ireland showed increase in the death rates due to homicide, which is contrary to the direction of general trend in other countries.

Indicator 16. Infant mortality rate

S-time-matrix: time when specified level of the indicator was achieved (sorted by last available value)

LEVEL	80	70	60	50	45	40	35	30	25	20	15	14	13	12	11	10	9	8	7	6	5	4	3	2
Slovenia							1960	1962	1971	1974	1980	1982	1985	1986	1987	1988	1989	1992	1993	1995	1998	2005	2007	**2012**
Finland										1962	1966	1969	1970	1972	1974	1975	1977	1978	1981	1989	1992	1998	**2005**	
Luxembourg							1962	1966	1971	1976	1977	1981	1982	1984	1985	1991	1992	1993	1993	2003	2011	**2012**		2008
Czech Republic										1971	1982	1984	1985	1987	1988	1992	1993	1994	1995	1996	1998	2003	**2007**	
Sweden											1963	1964	1968	1969	1971	1973	1975	1977	1983	1991	1993	1996	**2004**	
Greece						1962	1965	1970	1973	1977	1982	1985	1986	1986	1988	1989	1991	1995	1996	2000	2002	2004	**2012**	
Italy							1963	1966	1970	1973	1976	1980	1981	1982	1983	1984	1987	1989	1991	1993	1996	1999	2003	**2011**
Spain							1961	1965	1968	1970	1978	1979	1980	1981	1983	1985	1987	1988	1992	1994	1997	**2003**		
Austria							1961	1964	1972	1975	1978	1980	1981	1983	1985	1987	1987	1990	1993	1994	1996	**2005**		
France								1963	1969	1974	1975	1976	1976	1978	1980	1983	1986	1992	1994	1995	**2003**			
Germany					1960	1962	1965	1974	1977	1978	1979	1981	1982	1984	1985	1988	1990	1993	1996	**2005**				
Denmark										1962	1969	1970	1971	1972	1974	1976	1977	1989	1991	1993	2001	**2008**		
Portugal	1962	1964	1968	1971	1972	1974	1976	1977	1980	1982	1987	1987	1988	1989	1990	1992	1992	1994	1996	1998	2002	2003	**2011**	
Cyprus						1961	1964	1966	1971	1974	1978	1986	1988	1991	1992	1992	1993	1997	1998	1999	2001	**2005**		
Ireland							1961	1966	1970	1978	1978	1979	1979	1980	1983	1985	1990	1992	2000	2003	**2005**			
Croatia			1960	1962	1965	1966	1968	1970	1971	1974	1980	1986	1987	1988	1989	1992	1994	1995	1998	2002	2004	2009	**2012**	
Estonia							1960	1964	1966	1994	1995	1995	1996	1996	1997	2000	2001	2003	2004	2008	2009	**2011**		
Netherlands											1964	1967	1969	1971	1974	1977	1979	1985	1990	1993	2002	**2007**		
Belgium								1960	1964	1971	1976	1977	1978	1980	1982	1984	1988	1993	1994	1995	1999	**2006**		
EU 28							1962	1964	1970	1976	1981	1983	1984	1987	1988	1991	1993	1994	1997	2000	2005	**2010**		
Lithuania							1963	1964	1965	1970	1993	1994	1995	1995	1996	1997	1999	2004	2006	2007	2010	**2012**		
United Kingdom										1965	1979	1980	1981	1983	1985	1986	1988	1990	1992	1996	**2006**			
Poland				1964	1965	1966	1970	1971	1981	1988	1994	1995	1995	1996	1997	1997	1999	2000	2003	2007	**2010**			
Hungary				1963	1964	1971	1976	1978	1985	1991	1992	1993	1994	1995	1997	2000	2001	2003	2005	**2011**				
Malta							1962	1966	1971	1974	1980	1985	1985	1986	1986	1996	1996	2008	2009	**2011**	2006	2006		
Slovakia								1973	1981	1986	1987	1991	1992	1995	1996	1997	2000	2005	2008	**2011**				
Latvia										1963	1976	1998	1998	1999	1999	2001	2002	2004	2007	2009	**2010**			
Bulgaria				1960	1961	1963	1969	1974	1980	1998	2001	2002	2003	2005	2006	2010	**2012**							
Romania		1961	1962	1970	1971	1972	1974	1980	1990	1998	2005	2006	2006	2007	2008	2009	**2012**							

Infant mortality rate time matrix clearly shows enormous improvements in the last 50 years. The time matrix is divided into three parts with respect to the arrangement of the levels of the infant mortality rate. From the left steps are first changing by 10 values from values 80 to 50 to accommodate the presentation of large improvements in countries where starting values from the 1960's were above 50 (Portugal, Croatia, Poland, and Romania). From levels 50 to 15 the step was changing by 5 values, below 15 by value 1 to accommodate the presentation of additional progress done at best values.

Slovenia is having the lowest rate of infant mortality, followed by a group of six countries from Finland to Italy. However, the dynamics of improvement has been changing over time. For instance, the level of 10 was first reached By Sweden in 1973, followed by Finland in 1975, Denmark 1976, and Netherlands in 1977; Slovenia reached that level only in 1988 but accelerated the progress after that.

Indicator 17. At-risk-of-poverty (percent of total population)

S-time-matrix: time when specified level of the indicator was achieved (sorted by last available value)

LEVEL	26	25	24	23	22	21	20	19	18	17	16	15	14	13	12	11	10	9	8
Czech Republic																	2006	**2010**	2001
Netherlands														2003	**2011**	2007			
Denmark													**2011**	2008	2004	2001			
Finland													**2007**	2005	2004	1999	1998	1997	
Slovakia													**2011**	2010	2009				
Slovenia													**2010**	2010	2004	2003			
France										2000	2000	**2011**	2009	2003					
Sweden													**2011**	2010	2008	2007	2005	2001	1999
Hungary											2006	**2012**	2010	2003	2003	2002			
Austria												**2012**	2011	2009					
Cyprus										2005	**2011**								
Belgium										1995	**2012**	2002	2001						
Luxembourg												**2012**	2011	2004	2003	1997			
Malta												**2009**							
Ireland						2001	2005	2006	2006	2007	2008	**2009**							
Germany												**2012**	2007	2007	2006	2004	2001	2000	
United Kingdom							1995	2006	2009	**2010**									
EU 15											2004	**2007**	2003						
EU 28												**2012**							
Poland							2005	2006	2007	**2009**	2001								
Estonia							2004	2009	2009	**2011**	2010								
Portugal				1995	1997	2000	2004	2005	**2011**										
Lithuania								2010	**2011**	2002	2001								
Italy								1996	**2011**	2000									
Latvia	2009	2009	2009	2010	2010	2010	2010	**2011**	2003	2001	2000								
Croatia						**2011**	2010	2009	2009	2006									
Bulgaria					2011	2010	2006	2006	2006	2006	2005	2005	2005						
Spain					**2011**	2010	2007	2003	2000										
Romania			2008	2008	**2011**	2005	2005	2004	2004	2003									
Greece					**2012**	2011	2011	2010											

Eurostat is for recent years providing data on percentage of population at risk of poverty. The great diversity is obvious, from about 9-11 percent at the lower end of two best countries (Czech Republic and Netherlands) to about 23 percent in Greece, 22 percent in Romania, Bulgaria, Spain, and 21 percent in Croatia.

Unfortunately for majority of the countries the most recent values in bold are not the lowest values in the analysed period, i.e. rather more oriented on the left in the rows than to the right hand side. Only four countries in the middle showed clear improvement over time. Visually it is clear that the general tendency was towards increasing risk of poverty.

For a similar indicator 'At-risk-of-poverty or social exclusion' available time series are very short but the percentages of the risk are even higher.

Indicator 18. At-risk-of-poverty (percent of elderly population)

S-time-matrix: time when specified level of the indicator was achieved (sorted by last available value)

LEVEL	50	48	46	44	42	40	38	36	34	32	30	28	26	24	22	20	18	16	14	12	10	8	6	4
Hungary																				2001	2003	2006	**2012**	
Netherlands																						2009	**2012**	1998
Czech Republic																							**2012**	
Luxembourg																				1995	2003	2005	**2012**	
Slovakia																					2009	**2010**		
France																2000	2006	2007	2008	**2010**				
Ireland				2001	2002	2003	2004	2004	2005	2005	2005	2007	2007	2008	2008	2008	2009	2009	2009	2010	**2010**			
Poland																			**2012**	2008	2008	2007		
Denmark														2001	2002	2009	2010	**2011**						
EU 15																	1996	2009	**2011**					
EU 28																			**2010**					
Spain											2006	2008	2009	2009	2011	2011	**2012**	1996						
Germany																		**2007**	2006	2001	2000			
Austria														2001	2001	2002	2002	**2011**	2007					
Romania											2007	2008	2008	2008	2009	2009	2010	**2010**						
United Kingdom									1995	1996	1996	2008	2009	2009	2011	**2012**								
Italy																2006	2009	**2010**	2001	2000				
Estonia							2008	2009	2009	2009	2009	2009	2009	2010	2010	2010	2010	**2012**	2011					
Greece									1999	2002	2003	2005	2006	2007	2011	2012	**2012**							
Malta																2008	2009	2009	**2010**					
Portugal							1995	1998	1999	2000	2001	2005	2006	2007	2008	2011	**2012**							
Latvia	2008	2009	2009	2009	2009	2009	2009	2009	2009	2010	2010	2010	2010	2010	2010	2010	2010	**2013**	2012	2012	2011	2001	2000	
Sweden																		**2011**	2010	2008	2007	2007		
Belgium														2001	2002	2008	2011	**2012**						
Finland																	2009	**2010**	2005	1999	1998	1997		
Lithuania														2008	2009	2009	2009	2009	**2012**	2012	2011	2011	2011	
Slovenia																		**2012**						
Croatia										2004	2010	**2011**												
Bulgaria								2009	2009	2010	2010	**2011**	2007	2007	2007	2007	2006	2005	2004	2003				
Cyprus	2007	2008	2009	2009	2010	2010	2010	2011	2011	2012	**2012**													

Risk of poverty of elderly population is in general higher than the risk of poverty for total population. For elderly population the range of risk in the latest years is from 6 percent for Hungary, Netherlands, Czech Republic, and Luxembourg to the highest values of 30 percent Cyprus and Bulgaria, and 28 percent in Croatia. Data show that in Latvia and Cyprus the risk was even at the level of 50 percent in 2008 and 2007. For these two countries and for Ireland there was very considerable decrease in the risk of poverty of elderly population.

Though there were some deterioration in the current crisis this was not as overwhelming as in the case for the case of risk of poverty for total population. On the other hand, at the country level there are several case when the risk of poverty for elderly population is higher than that for total population and cases in the other direction. Detailed examination of individual cases is necessary.

Indicator 19. Income quintile share ratio S80/S20

S-time-matrix: time when specified level of the indicator was achieved (sorted by last available value)

LEVEL	7.8	7.6	7.4	7.2	7	6.8	6.6	6.4	6.2	6	5.8	5.6	5.4	5.2	5	4.8	4.6	4.4	4.2	4	3.8	3.6	3.4	3.2	3
Slovenia																							**2012**	2009	
Czech Republic																							2006	**2008**	
Netherlands																		1996	1996	2009	2011	**2012**			
Finland																				2008	**2010**	2000	1998	1997	
Slovakia																				2006	**2011**	2009	2008		
Sweden																					**2011**	2008	2000	1997	
Belgium																	1995	2006	**2009**						
Malta																	2000	2001	2010	**2011**					
Luxembourg																		2010	**2011**	2001	1997				
Austria																			**2012**	2012	2011	2001	2000		
Hungary													2006	2006	2006	2006	2007	2007	**2013**	2012	2011	2010	2010	2003	2002
Germany															2008	2009	**2012**	2006	2006	2005	2001				
Denmark																	2009	**2011**	2009	2008	2008	2008	2006	2002	2001
France																	**2011**	2010	2008	2007	2003				
Ireland													1998	2005	2007	**2011**	2009	2009							
Cyprus																	**2012**	2011	2004						
Poland							2005	2005	2005	2006	2006	2006	2007	2008	**2011**	2001									
EU 15															**2010**	2007	2003								
EU 28															**2010**										
Lithuania			2010	2010	2010	2010	2011	2011	2011	2011	2011	**2012**	2002	2001											
Croatia												**2012**	2010	2010	2009	2009	2009								
Estonia			2004	2004	2004	2004	2005	2005	2005	2005	2006	**2012**	2011	2010											
United Kingdom											2005	2008	**2012**	2000	1998	1997									
Italy											1995	**2011**	2011	2010	2002	2001									
Portugal			2003	2004	2005	2006	2007	2007	2008	2009	**2012**	2010													
Bulgaria							2007	2007	2008	2011	**2012**	2010	2006	2006	2006	2006	2006	2006	2006	2005	2005	2005	2003		
Latvia	2006	2006	2009	2009	2010	2010	2011	**2013**	2003	2002	2001	2000													
Romania	2007	2007	2008	2008	2008	2009	2009	2009	**2011**	2010	2006	2006	2006	2006	2005	2004	2003								
Greece												**2012**	2012	2011	2011	2011	2010								
Spain				**2012**	2010	2010	2009	2009	2009	2008	2008	2008	2005	2004											

The income inequality is measured by two indicators; one of them is Income quintile share ratio S80/S20. The range between countries is again very large, from ratio of 3.4 in best countries Slovenia and Czech Republic to more than twice higher ratio of 7.2 in Spain. We have only six countries with the ratio below 4: Slovenia, Czech Republic, Netherlands, Finland, Slovakia, and Sweden. There were 13 countries with ratio 5 or above: Poland, Lithuania, Croatia, Estonia, United Kingdom, Italy, Portugal, Bulgaria, Latvia, Romania, Greece, and Spain; a strange mixture of EU15 countries and later accessions.

Again, also for the income inequality the situation worsened in the recent years, with only about three exceptions. Spain and Greece at the bottom of the matrix are showing very strong deterioration, but there were also deterioration in some higher income EU countries.

Indicator 20. GINI coefficient

S-time-matrix: time when specified level of the indicator was achieved (sorted by last available value)

LEVEL	38	37	36	35	34	33	32	31	30	29	28	27	26	25	24	23	22	21	20
Slovenia																2009	2003		
Sweden															2008	2004	1999	1997	
Czech Republic													2005	2012					
Slovakia											2006	2006	2007	2009	2008				
Netherlands										2000	2001	2009	2010	1998					
Finland												2001	2009	2000	2000	1999	1998		
Belgium									2000	2001	2005	2008							
Malta									2000	2002	2010	2007							
Austria												2012	2010	2002	2001				
Hungary						2006	2006	2006	2006	2007	2013	2012	2011	2010	2002				
Luxembourg										2009	2012	2005	2000	1997					
Denmark											2012	2010	2009	2007	2006	2002	2001	1999	1997
Germany									2008	2011	2006	2006	2005	2001					
Ireland					1998	1999	1999	2007	2011	2009									
Croatia								2011	2010	2009	2009	2009							
France									2010	2008	2007	2007							
EU 28									2010										
EU 15								1995	2007	2001									
Poland				2005	2006	2006	2008	2012	2001										
Cyprus								2012	2011	2008	2004	2003							
Italy						2005	2007	2008	2002	2001									
Lithuania		2010	2010	2011	2011	2011	2012	2001											
Estonia		2004	2004	2005	2005	2007	2011	2008											
United Kingdom				2002	2005	2011	2000	1998	1997										
Romania		2007	2008	2009	2010	2006	2006	2005	2003	2000									
Bulgaria				2011	2012	2006	2006	2006	2006	2006	2005	2005	2005	2005	2003				
Greece				1998	2012	2010													
Portugal	2005	2007	2008	2009	2011														
Spain				2012	2010	2009	2008	2004											
Latvia	2006	2009	2010	2002	2000														

The income inequality is measured also by the Gini coefficient. The range between countries is again very large, from the lowest value of 0.23 in Slovenia to the highest values in the range of 0.33-0.36 from United Kingdom, Romania, Bulgaria, Greece, Portugal, Spain, and Latvia. The six best countries with income quintile ratio below 4: Slovenia, Czech Republic, Netherlands, Finland, Slovakia, and Sweden are in the range of 0.23-0.26 confirming the lowest income inequality.

Again, also for Gini coefficient indicator of the income inequality the situation worsened in the recent years, with only about three examples. The detrimental effect of the world financial and socio-economic system on the GDP level and on the GDP growth rate, that is in the focus in the literature and in media, is observed and felt even with greater intensity in the deterioration of employment rates, investment share in the GDP, in the increasing risk of poverty and increasing income inequality.

Indicator 21. Early leavers from education and training

S-time-matrix: time when specified level of the indicator was achieved (sorted by last available value)

LEVEL	50	48	46	44	42	40	38	36	34	32	30	28	26	24	22	20	18	16	14	12	10	8	6	4
Croatia																						2002	2004	**2013**
Slovenia																							**2001**	
Czech Republic																							**2005**	
Poland																							**2003**	
Lithuania																2000	2002	2003	2004	**2010**				
Luxembourg					1992	1992	1993	1993	1996	1997	1997	1997	1998	1998	1999	1999	2001	2002	2006	2008	2009	**2012**		
Slovakia																						**2013**		
Sweden																				2005	**2007**			
Austria																			1996	2008	**2011**			
Denmark																			1992	2008	**2011**	1995		
Ireland													1992	1993	1995	1996	1998	2000	2002	2006	**2012**			
Netherlands																		1999	2004	2007	**2010**			
Finland																					**2011**	1998		
Cyprus														2004	2005	2006	2006	2011	**2013**					
Germany																		2000	2008	**2013**				
Greece															1994	1995	1998	2000	2003	2010	**2012**			
Estonia																				2008	**2010**			
Latvia																		2003	2004	2009	**2011**			
Belgium																		1992	1994	2003	**2012**			
France																			1994	2000	**2011**			
Hungary																			1998	1999	**2007**			
EU 28																			2004	2010	**2013**			
Bulgaria																	2005	2006	2007	2010	**2011**			
United Kingdom									1993	1994	1994	1995	1996	1997	1997	1998	1999	2001	2009	**2012**	2006			
EU 15															1995	1995	1999	1999	2003	2009	**2012**			
Italy							1994	1994	1996	1997	1998	2000	2002	2005	2007	**2011**								
Romania																	2004	2005	2010	2008				
Portugal	1992	1993	1998	2002	2003	2004	2007	2008	2008	2009	2009	2010	2010	2011	2012	**2013**								
Malta	2003	2003	2004	2004	2004	2004	2004	2005	2005	2007	2008	2009	2010	2011	**2012**									
Spain						1992	1993	1994	1995	2004	2009	2010	**2011**											

Early leavers from education and training as percentage of the age group 18-24 years show the stability of the education and training system in offering the opportunities to younger generation in this respect. The best performers are Croatia by around 4 percent, closely followed by Slovenia, Czech Republic, Poland, and Slovakia at around 6 percent. On the other side of the range there was Spain with 26, Malta with 22, and Portugal with 20 percent.

In a large group of 15 countries the share of early leavers did not fall below 10 percent, including very large EU15 countries as France, United Kingdom, Italy, and Spain. However, the trends have been favourable, with three small exceptions we can see the moment to the right in the rows indicating continuous decrease in the share of early leavers. This trend is different than the worsening situation with employment and inequality trends.

Indicator 22. Healthy life years at birth - females

S-time-matrix: time when specified level of the indicator was achieved (sorted by last available value)

LEVEL	53	54	55	56	57	58	59	60	61	62	63	64	65	66	67	68	69	70	71	72	73	74
Malta														2002	2003	2003	2004	2006	2011	**2012**		
Sweden								1997	2004	2005	2005	2005	2005	2006	2007	2008	2008	2009	**2010**			
Ireland												2005	2008	2009	2010	**2011**						
Luxembourg									2004	2005	2006	2007	2008	2009	**2011**							
Bulgaria														**2011**	2010	2008	2008	2007	2007	2007	2007	
Spain										2009	2010	**2011**	2004	2003	2003	2003	2003					
Belgium							2004	2004	2005	2005	2010	2011	**2012**	2003	2003	2003	2003					
Greece													**2012**	2011	2011	2006	1999					
Croatia									2010	2011	2011	**2012**										
United Kingdom									2003	2003	2004	2004	**2011**	2009								
Czech Republic								2006	2006	2007	2009	**2012**										
Cyprus							2005	2005	2011	2011	2012	**2012**	2009	2004	2003	2003	2003					
France										1998	**2009**											
Poland									2007	**2012**	2006	2005	2005	2005	2003							
Austria								2008	2011	**2012**	2004	2004	2004	2003	2003	2003	2003					
EU 28										**2012**												
Lithuania			2005	2006	2006	2007	2007	2008	2009	**2011**												
Italy										**2012**	2011	2011	2011	2010	2010	2005	2005	2004	2004	2004	2003	2003
Denmark								2011	**2012**	2008	2008	2008	2007	2007	2007	2005	2004					
Hungary			2005	2006	2006	2007	2011	**2012**														
Latvia	2006	2007	2008	2009	2011	2012	**2012**															
Netherlands								2011	2010	2008	2008	2007	2007									
Portugal	2004	2004	2005	2005	2010	**2011**	2003	2003	2003	2002	1995											
Germany			2005	2005	2006	**2012**	2004	2004	2004	2004	2003	2003										
Romania					2011	2010	2010	2009	2009	2009												
Estonia	2005	2006	2007	2007	2008	**2011**	2009															
Finland	2006	2006	2006	2007	**2012**	2011	2009															
Slovenia			2011	**2012**	2010	2010	2010	2009	2009	2009	2007											
Slovakia	**2012**	2008	2007	2007																		

Healthy life years at birth intend to add also the information on number of years that a person is expected to live in a healthy condition. It combines information both on the quality and length of life for newly born population (as well as for elderly population in another indicator for healthy life years at the age of 65). Eurostat considers that comparisons between countries might be influenced by cultural differences so without going into details the comparisons over time are more relevant.

In such comparisons over time for a given country there were 10 countries where the indicator was improving in the sense that the most recent value in bold was the highest level achieved. In the other 18 countries the direction of change in the last year(s) was in the direction of lowering the healthy life years for females. In most of these countries these deteriorations were again very much related to the period of the recent depression.

Indicator 23. Healthy life years at birth - males

S-time-matrix: time when specified level of the indicator was achieved (sorted by last available value)

LEVEL	49	50	51	52	53	54	55	56	57	58	59	60	61	62	63	64	65	66	67	68	69	70	71
Malta																		2003	2004	2004	2008	2010	**2011**
Sweden														2004	2004	2005	2005	2006	2006	2007	2008	2008	**2012**
Ireland															2007	2009	2010	**2011**					
Luxembourg												2004	2005	2007	2007	2008	**2010**						
Greece															2004	**2012**	2011						
Spain															2009	2010	**2012**	2003					
United Kingdom													1999	2003	2004	2005	**2011**						
Belgium												2004	2004	2005	2005	2006	**2012**	2003	2003	2003			
Netherlands														2010	2011	**2011**	2007	2007					
Cyprus												2005	2005	2011	**2012**	2010	2010	2004	2003	2003			
France												1999	2003	**2010**									
Czech Republic										2006	2006	2007	2007	**2010**									
Bulgaria															2010	2008	2007	2007	2007				
Italy															**2011**	2011	2011	2010	2010	2004	2004	2003	
Croatia										2010	2011	2011	2012	**2012**									
EU 28													2010										
Portugal								2004	2005	2005	2010	**2011**											
Denmark														**2012**	2012	2011	2008	2007	2007	2007	2006		
Austria											2009	**2012**	2004	2004	2003	2003	2003	2003					
Hungary					2005	2006	2008	2009	2011	2011	**2012**												
Poland											2007	**2011**	2005	2005	2003								
Romania											2010	2009	2009										
Germany							2005	2005	**2009**	2007	2007	2004	2004	2004	2003	2003	2003						
Finland				2005	2006	2006	2007	2007	2007	**2011**													
Lithuania				2006	2006	2007	2008	2009	**2011**														
Slovenia						2011	2011	**2012**	2010	2009	2009	2009											
Latvia			2007	2008	2009	**2011**																	
Slovakia					**2012**	2007	2007																
Estonia	2006	2007	2007	2008	2008	**2011**	2009																

Discussing the situation for healthy life years for males we follow the Eurostat comment above that comparisons between countries might be influenced by cultural differences and therefore we shall concentrate on comments about the comparisons over time rather than that between countries.

In such comparisons over time for males there were 13 countries where the indicator was improving in the sense that the most recent value in bold was the highest level achieved in the analysed period. In the other 15 countries the direction of change in the last year(s) was in the direction of lowering the healthy life years for males, in most of these countries the deterioration happened again in the period of crisis.

The situation with respect to healthy life years for female and males in an important way adjusts the view of continuous improvements in the life expectancy in indicator 1 to consider also the decrease in the healthy life expectancy for both females and males especially in some years of the crisis.

Indicator 24. Households with broadband access

S-time-matrix: time when specified level of the indicator was achieved (sorted by last available value)

LEVEL	3	8	13	18	23	28	33	38	43	48	53	58	63	68	73	78	83	88
Finland			2003	2004	2004	2004	2005	2005	2005	2006	2006	2007	2007	2008	2009	2010	2012	2013
Denmark						2003	2004	2004	2004	2005	2005	2006	2006	2007	2008	2010	2011	
Netherlands					2003	2004	2004	2004	2005	2005	2005	2005	2006	2006	2007	2009	2011	
Sweden									2005	2006	2006	2006	2007	2007	2008	2009	2010	
United Kingdom			2003	2004	2004	2005	2005	2006	2006	2006	2007	2007	2008	2009	2010	2011	2012	
Germany			2003	2004	2005	2005	2006	2006	2007	2007	2008	2008	2009	2009	2010	2011	2012	
Austria			2004	2004	2005	2006	2006	2006	2007	2007	2008	2009	2010	2011	2011	2012		
Belgium									2005	2006	2007	2008	2009	2010	2011	2013		
Estonia						2004	2005	2005	2006	2007	2007	2008	2009	2010	2011	2012	2013	
Malta						2005	2005	2006	2006	2007	2007	2008	2008	2009	2010	2011	2013	
EU 15				2004	2005	2005	2006	2006	2007	2007	2008	2009	2010	2011	2012	2013		
France						2006	2006	2007	2007	2008	2008	2009	2011	2011	2013			
EU 28									2007	2008	2009	2009	2010	2011	2012			
Slovenia			2004	2005	2005	2006	2006	2006	2007	2008	2009	2009	2010	2011	2012			
Hungary		2004	2005	2006	2006	2007	2007	2008	2008	2009	2010	2011	2011	2012				
Latvia		2004	2005	2005	2006	2007	2007	2008	2008	2009	2010	2011	2012	2012				
Luxembourg		2003	2004	2004	2004	2005	2005	2005	2006	2006	2007	2007	2008	2012				
Slovakia		2005	2006	2006	2007	2007	2008	2008	2009	2010	2011	2011	2011	2012				
Czech Republic	2004	2005	2006	2006	2007	2007	2008	2008	2009	2009	2010	2010	2012	2013				
Poland		2004	2005	2005	2006	2007	2007	2008	2008	2009	2009	2010	2011	2013				
Spain			2005	2005	2006	2006	2007	2008	2009	2009	2010	2011	2013					
Italy			2005	2006	2007	2008	2008	2009	2009	2010	2011	2012	2013	2013				
Ireland	2004	2005	2006	2006	2007	2007	2007	2008	2008	2008	2009	2010	2011					
Croatia						2007	2008	2009	2009	2009	2010	2011	2012	2013				
Cyprus	2005	2006	2006	2007	2007	2008	2008	2008	2009	2009	2010	2011	2013					
Lithuania	2004	2005	2005	2006	2006	2007	2007	2007	2008	2009	2010	2012	2013					
Portugal		2003	2004	2005	2006	2007	2007	2008	2009	2010	2010	2011						
Romania		2007	2008	2008	2010	2011	2011	2011	2012	2012	2013							
Greece	2006	2007	2007	2008	2008	2009	2009	2010	2011	2012	2013							
Bulgaria		2005	2007	2008	2008	2010	2011	2011	2011	2012	2013							

The percentage of household with broadband access as one of the ICT indicators shows the very important characteristic of extremely high dynamics in this field. In the leading country Finland the share of households with this access increased from about 13 percent in 2003 to 88 percent in 2013, i.e. in a single decade. The much higher growth rate of increase than that in the indicators from other domains means that some high static measures for evaluation of differences between countries do not tell the whole story. The static ratio in 2013 between Finland, on one hand, and Romania, Greece, and Bulgaria, on the other, of 1.66 (88/53) must be accompanied by time distance assessment that at level of 53 percent of access Finland had only 7 years of time lead (2006 vs. 2013). The perception of the degree of disparity is rather different if one uses the measures of 66 percent or 7 years. For realistic assessment we need both static and time distance measures.

Indicator 25. Regular Internet use

S-time-matrix: time when specified level of the indicator was achieved (sorted by last available value)

LEVEL	10	15	20	25	30	35	40	45	50	55	60	65	70	75	80	85	90
Luxembourg									2003	2004	2004	2006	2007	2008	2009	2010	**2012**
Netherlands														2006	2007	2009	**2011**
Sweden													2003	2007	2008	2009	**2011**
Denmark												2003	2004	2005	2008	2010	**2013**
Finland											2003	2005	2006	2007	2009	**2011**	
United Kingdom								2004	2005	2006	2007	2008	2009	2010	**2012**		
Belgium										2005	2006	2008	2009	2010	**2013**		
Germany							2003	2004	2005	2006	2007	2009	2010	**2013**			
France							2006	2006	2007	2007	2008	2009	2010	**2011**			
Austria							2003	2004	2005	2006	2007	2008	2010	**2011**			
Estonia								2004	2005	2006	2007	2009	2010	**2012**			
EU 15							2004	2005	2006	2007	2008	2009	2011	**2013**			
Ireland				2003	2005	2005	2006	2006	2007	2008	2009	2010	2011	**2013**			
Slovakia							2004	2006	2007	2007	2008	2009	**2010**				
EU 28										2008	2009	2010	**2012**				
Hungary				2004	2005	2005	2006	2006	2007	2008	2010	2011	**2013**				
Latvia					2004	2005	2005	2006	2007	2008	2009	2011	**2012**				
Czech Republic			2003	2004	2005	2006	2007	2007	2008	2009	2010	2012	**2013**				
Slovenia							2004	2005	2006	2007	2009	2009	**2012**				
Malta							2006	2007	2008	2008	2009	2010	**2011**				
Spain						2004	2005	2006	2007	2008	2009	2011	**2012**				
Lithuania				2003	2004	2005	2006	2006	2007	2008	2009	2011	**2013**				
Croatia							2007	2008	2009	2010	2011	**2012**					
Cyprus						2006	2008	2009	2009	2010	2011	**2013**					
Poland					2004	2005	2006	2007	2008	2009	2010	**2013**					
Portugal						2004	2006	2007	2009	2010	2011	**2012**					
Greece		2003	2005	2006	2007	2008	2010	2011	2012	**2013**							
Italy			2003	2006	2007	2009	2010	2011	**2013**								
Bulgaria		2004	2006	2007	2007	2008	2009	2011	**2012**								
Romania	2004	2005	2007	2008	2009	2010	2012	**2013**									

The indicator of regular Internet use is more demanding as it goes beyond the mere availability of new technology. Yet it possesses the similar characteristic of very high growth rates.

The leading Scandinavian countries started with much higher values in the range above 60 percent already in about 2004 when Romania was still at 10 percent and Bulgaria, Greece were at 15 percent and Italy at 20 percent. So even if Romania from 2004 to 2013 increased the share nearly fivefold the time lag is more substantial than in the case of households with Internet access.

The interesting point is that some of the countries from EU15 are positioned low in the matrix: Italy, Greece, Portugal, and Spain from the southern part as against the others positioned in the first 9. Several countries from the 2004 widening have positioned themselves between these two EU15 groups.

Indicator 26. Share of energy from renewable sources

S-time-matrix: time when specified level of the indicator was achieved (sorted by last available value)

LEVEL	0	2	4	6	8	10	12	14	16	18	20	22	24	26	28	30	32	34	36	38	40	42	44	46	48	50
Sweden																					2005	2006	2007	2008	2011	**2012**
Latvia																2008	2008	**2011**								
Finland																2007	2010	**2012**								
Austria													2005	2006	2008	2009	**2012**									
Denmark									2006	2007	2009	2010	2011	**2012**												
Estonia										2008	2008	2009	**2010**													
Portugal											2005	2007	**2009**													
Romania										2007	2008	**2011**														
Lithuania										2008	**2011**															
Slovenia										2008	2009	**2012**														
Croatia								2010	**2011**																	
Bulgaria						2007	2009	2010	**2012**																	
Spain						2007	2009	**2012**																		
EU 28						2007	2009	**2012**																		
Greece					2008	2010	**2011**																			
Italy				2005	2008	2010	**2011**																			
France						2007	**2011**																			
Germany				2004	2006	2009	**2012**																			
Czech Republic				2005	2008	**2011**																				
Poland					2008	**2011**																				
Slovakia				2006	2008	**2011**																				
Hungary				2007	**2009**																					
Ireland			2008	**2010**																						
Belgium		2004	2009	**2012**																						
Cyprus			2007	**2011**																						
Netherlands		2004	**2011**																							
United Kingdom		2007	**2012**																							
Luxembourg		**2006**																								
Malta	**2004**																									

Share of energy from renewable sources allows a quick glimpse at the great differences in this respect, partly due to availability of natural resources and partly to policy differences.

Apart from the exceptional share in Sweden, the range is extraordinary from a few percent to more than 30 percent of the renewable sources. It is interesting to observe that many large countries are positioned below the halve of this range: Spain at 14 percent, Italy, France, and Germany at 12 percent, Poland at 10, United Kingdom even at about 4 percent.

It will be very difficult for the general EU orientation towards renewable sources and the targets set in the National Reform Programmes (NRPs) to overcome these gaps. The need is obvious but the rate of change in the past and the wide range of situations seen at a glance in the matrix does not look very promising if further operational programs are not put in place and executed.

Indicator 27. Urban population exposure to air pollution by particulate matter PM10

S-time-matrix: time when specified level of the indicator was achieved (sorted by last available value)

LEVEL	60	58	56	54	52	50	48	46	44	42	40	38	36	34	32	30	28	26	24	22	20	18	16	14	12
Denmark																		2006	2007	2008	2008	2009	2009	2010	**2010**
Finland																						1999	2008	**2011**	
Estonia																			2006	2007	2007	2007	**2010**	2009	
Sweden																			2006	2008	**2011**	2010			
Ireland																			2003	2003	**2011**	2010	2009		
Luxembourg																				2006	**2011**	2010	2009		
United Kingdom																1997	1998	2003	2007	2008	**2011**	2010			
Germany																		2003	2006	2007	**2009**				
Latvia																				**2010**	2010	2009			
Lithuania																		2000	2010	**2011**	2009	2008			
Spain					1998	1998	1999	1999	2000	2000	2006	2007	2007	2008	2009	**2010**									
EU 15														1997	1997	2003	2007	**2011**							
France																		**2009**	2008	2006	2005				
Netherlands													1999	2003	2006	2007	2008	**2009**							
Austria																	2001	2006	2006	**2010**	2009	2008			
Belgium										1997	1997	2003	2004	2004	2006	**2010**	2008								
EU 28															1997	2006	2007	**2010**							
Portugal											1999	1999	1999	2004	2005	2007	2008	**2010**							
Czech Republic										2003	2003	2004	2006	2006	2007	**2010**	2009	2008							
Slovenia									2003	2004	2004	2005	2005	2006	2007	**2011**	2010								
Italy								2000	2000	2000	2006	2007	2007	2008	**2011**	2010									
Hungary														2006	2006	2007	**2011**	2009	2004	2004	2004				
Slovakia														1999	**2011**	2011	2010	2010	2009						
Cyprus						2010	2010	2010	2011	2011	2011	**2011**													
Poland					1998	1998	1998	1998	1999	2006	2006	**2010**	2009	2009	2008										
Romania				2004	2006	2006	2007	2007	2007	2008	2008	**2011**	2010	2010	2009	2009									
Bulgaria	2008	**2011**	2011	2011	2010	2010	2010	2002	2002	2002	2002	2002	2001	2001	2001	2001	2001	2001	2000	2000	2000				
China	**2009**																								
India	2007	2009	2009	2010	**2010**																				

Important indicator in the domain of environment is exposure of urban population to air pollution by particulate matter PM10. Data relate to urban-population weighted PM10 levels in residential areas of cities with more than 100,000 residents. Again, there are huge differences between countries.

The column in red for the level of PM10 concentrations 20 micrograms per cubic metre shows the level of WHO recommended annual level. The matrix clearly shows that many countries are still above that level. In the recent years only seven EU countries were at this or lower levels, 21 EU countries are not meeting such recommendation.

Many other comparisons between countries and their dynamics can be made, both within EU and beyond. This pollution is much higher in China and India than in any EU country except Bulgaria.

Indicator 28. Publications per million inhabitants

S-time-matrix: time when specified level of the indicator was achieved (sorted by last available value)

LEVEL	500	1000	1500	2000	2500	3000	3500	4000	4500	5000	5500	6000	6500	7000	7500	8000	8500	9000	9500	10000	10500	11000
Denmark												1995	1997	1999	2002	2004	2006	2007	2008	2008	2009	2010
Sweden													1995	1997	1999	2002	2004	2006	2008	2009		
Netherlands										1994	1997	2001	2003	2004	2006	2007	2008	2009				
Finland											1995	1996	1998	2000	2003	2005	2007	2008				
Slovenia				1995	1997	1998	2000	2001	2003	2004	2005	2006	2007	2008	2008	2009						
Belgium							1996	1998	2001	2003	2005	2006	2008	2009								
United										1995	1997	2003	2005	2007	2009							
Ireland					1996	2000	2002	2004	2005	2006	2007	2008	2008	2009								
Austria						1996	1998	2000	2003	2005	2007	2008	2010									
Germany						1995	1998	2004	2007	2010												
Luxembourg		2000	2003	2005	2006	2007	2008	2008	2009	2010												
Spain			1996	2000	2003	2005	2007	2008	2010													
France						1996	2003	2007														
Estonia			1995	1998	2003	2005	2006	2008	2009													
Greece			1995	1998	2001	2003	2005	2006	2008													
Portugal		1997	2000	2002	2004	2006	2007	2009	2010													
EU 27				1994	1999	2005	2008															
Czech			1995	1998	2003	2005	2007	2008														
Italy				1998	2002	2005	2008															
Cyprus	1994	1998	2003	2005	2007	2008	2009	2010														
Lithuania	1995	2002	2004	2005	2007	2008																
Hungary				1999	2005																	
Slovakia			1995	2004	2008																	
Poland			1996	2002	2006	2009																
Malta	1996	2006	2009																			
Romania	2002	2007	2010																			
Bulgaria			2010																			
Latvia		2008																				

Scientific publications per million of inhabitants intend to bring into the picture also the performance in the scientific domain. In this matrix data are from ARRS (2014), Time Matrix for Publications per Million Inhabitants in 5-year Periods, based on ISI database Web of Science, 2013. The differences between EU countries are large from Denmark with about 11000 publications to 1000 in Latvia and 1500 in Malta, Romania, and Bulgaria.

The time matrix shows clear trend toward higher number of publications, one of the greatest dynamics was in Slovenia with 12 steps from 2000 in 1995 to 8000 in 2009, similar dynamics was achieved in Denmark with 11 steps, followed by Ireland, Luxemburg, Spain, Estonia, Greece, Portugal, and Cyprus.

Indicator 29. Proportion of seats in national parliaments held by women

S-time-matrix: time when specified level of the indicator was achieved (sorted by last available value)

LEVEL	6	8	10	12	14	16	18	20	22	24	26	28	30	32	34	36	38	40	42	44	46
Sweden																				2003	**2010**
Finland																	2006	2010	**2011**		
Denmark																	**2011**				
Netherlands																2002	2008	**2011**			
Belgium										2003	2003	2003	2004	2004	2004	2009	**2013**				
Germany														2008	2012	**2013**					
Spain									2000	2000	2001	2004	2004	2005	2005	**2013**					
Austria													2012	2012	**2013**	2004					
Slovenia		2000	2001	2004	2010	2011	2011	2011	2011	2012	2012	2012	2012	**2012**							
Italy			2002	2005	2005	2006	2007	2008	2012	2012	2012	2013	**2013**								
Portugal							2002	2004	2007	2007	2008	2012	**2013**								
Luxembourg							2004	2011	2011	2012	2012	**2013**									
France					2004	2006	2007	2007	2011	2011	2012	**2012**									
Poland					2001	2001	2002	2011	**2012**												
United Kingdom							2004	2009	**2011**												
Greece	2000	2001	2004	2005	2006	2010	2011	**2012**													
Estonia							2003	**2012**	2010												
Czech Republic						2009	2009	**2013**	2012												
Slovak Republic					2002	2011	**2013**	2006													
Ireland				2002	**2010**																
Hungary		2002	**2010**																		

As an example of time matrix presentation and visualisation for gender disparities the indicator 'Proportion of seats in national parliaments held by women' is shown. It is very easy to understand and can be used for other indicators describing the share of women in several fields, like employment, women in science, etc.

In the EU differences are huge, from 46 percent in Sweden to 10 percent in Hungary. From the same data set from OECDStatExtracts immediately behind Sweden South Africa is placed at 44 percent, India, Hungary, and Japan at 10 percent and Brazil at 8 percent were very far away from that.

With normal variation at new changes of parliaments the general trend is towards higher portion of seats held by women. The greatest increase was in Slovenia from 8 to 32 percent, Italy from 10 to 30, by 7 steps of 2 percent the proportion was increased in Belgium, Italy, Spain, France, and Greece. But in six EU countries the proportion did not increase above 20 percent (Hungary, Ireland, Slovakia, Czech Republic, Estonia, and Greece). United Kingdom and Poland were above that but below one quarter.

Indicator 30. Current account balance in percent of GDP

S-time-matrix: time when specified level of the indicator was achieved (sorted by last available value)

LEVEL	-24	-22	-20	-18	-16	-14	-12	-10	-8	-6	-4	-2	0	2	4	6	8	10	12	14	16
Netherlands													1980	2000	2002	2009	2010	**2013**			
Germany													2001	2003	2004	**2009**					
Denmark											1987	1988	1998	2007	2009	**2012**					
Slovenia											2008	2009	2010	2012	2012	**2013**					
Sweden														1995	1999	**2012**	2008				
Luxembourg																**2012**	2007	2007	2000		
Ireland											2008	2009	2010	2011	**2012**						
Hungary							1994	2005	2008	2008	2009	2010	**2013**								
Austria											1998	2001	**2012**	2008							
Slovakia								2006	2008	2009	2011	2012	**2012**	1994							
Bulgaria	2008	2008	2008	2008	2009	2009	2009	2009	2009	2009	2010	2010	**2012**	1998	1997						
Lithuania						2007	2008	2008	2008	2008	2009	2011	**2012**	2009							
Malta						2000	2000	2009	2010	2010	2011	2011	**2012**								
Croatia									2008	2009	2009	2010	**2012**								
Italy												2011	**2012**	1998							
Spain								2007	2008	2009	2011	2012	**2013**								
Greece						2008	2009	2011	2011	2012	2012	2012	**2013**								
Portugal							2008	2010	2011	2011	2012	2012	**2013**								
Latvia		2007	2007	2007	2008	2008	2008	2008	2008	2008	2008	2008	**2012**	2011	2010	2010	2009	2009	1994	1993	1993
Estonia						2007	2008	2008	2008	2008	2008	2009	**2012**	2011							
Finland										1975	1992	1993	**2011**	2009	2007	2004	2002				
Romania		1994	1994	1994	1994	1994	1994	2008	2008	2008	2009	2012	**2013**								
France													**2012**	2005	1999						
Poland											2008	2012	**2013**	1995							
Czech Republic											2003	2007	**2012**	1993							
Belgium													**2011**	2005	2002						
Cyprus						2008	2009	2010	2010	2012	2013	**2013**	1999	1998							
United Kingdom											**2012**	2011	1985								

This indicator is an example of many other indicators in the economic domain that could be presented by the S-time-matrix. There are two main groups of countries in this respect. One set of countries were over the analysed period keeping the tendency towards higher share of current balance; the other group of countries showed a quite different story of considerable variation over time. There were also differences in the length of available data series and how different countries behaved before and after the start of the recent depression.

Approximately for the most recent values the greatest concentration is around level 0, which means balanced current account. At that level were 10 countries, many of them coming from the left side of the matrix by realising that such huge current account deficits are not sustainable (about 11 countries were in the column with value of -10 in the past, a deficit that requires change in only one direction). With the highest recent values on the positive side are Netherlands at 10 percent, Germany, Denmark, Slovenia, Sweden, and Luxembourg at 6 percent.

CONCLUSIONS

There are three salient points streaming from the broad journey through the 30 indicators to unravel the portrait of the EU and the EU countries.

1. The first point is methodological: it is very important how people understand data and indicators. For that we need beyond data also innovative concepts of looking at data and new generic statistical measures in order to better perceive and exploit the information available in existing data. Static measures of disparity and percentage growth rates of the present state-of-the-art alone are not enough to describe the broader dynamic reality. **Time distance is an innovative approach** for looking at time series data. Expressed in time units, the approach is easy to understand and provides a useful complement to existing methods. The strength of the time distance concept is that it enables additional exploitation of data and clear visualization of time series. **It is a generic concept, in the same way as static difference and growth rates; it provides an additional view to many problems and applications.**

Seeing with new eyes, to borrow the phrase from Marcel Proust, creates new knowledge and better understanding also for social and economic phenomena. **Both beyond GDP initiatives and beyond static statistical measures are two directions of seeing with new eyes**, which can complement each other. In this study it was shown how to present and visualise indicators over time with the novel level-time matrix and how to measure intertemporal changes in composite indicators like Human Development Index. It was this innovative time matrix presentation that enabled condensed summary visual presentation over many countries and over time for the 30 selected indicators. Under each time matrix a brief comment offers some possible introductory interpretation of the situation of the indicator. **Many other comparisons of levels between countries and their dynamics in the matrix can be made by imaginative users.**

Last but not least, in the **Annex A1 Time Matrix Calculator** is provided to calculate time matrix to **enable users to test and analyse their own data in time matrix format. There is no need to collect new data: one can start using existing data and indicators systems** from international, national, regional, business, and local sources.

2. The second point relates to the degree of disparities in the level and dynamics of the selected indicators in the EU. **Both visually and in numbers it was shown that very large differences exist between countries in both respects – levels and dynamics.** In the perception of the overall situation in the EU in various domains and in the policy considerations this should be kept in mind at all times. Overall the general policy orientation and policy instruments should be regulated to the circumstances at the starting situation and to the vision of future economic and social development in a given country. As these conditions are so varied it must be clearly understood that this is a very complex problem to be dealt with. Also the European Commission and European Parliament should expect that over-regulation in some domains will be ineffective and inefficient.

3. An important point relates to the **multidimensional nature of development and well-being, especially in relation to the effects of the world financial crisis**. One of them is that the damage done to individual EU countries by the world financial crisis is seen in different dimensions and scale of the damage when we look for 28 countries beyond GDP and consider also deterioration in employment rate, investment share, risk of poverty, income distribution, health, etc.

While media and also official organizations are focusing on discussion of GDP growth rate (even discussing changes in this rate of e.g. 0.2 percent over quarters or years as the sign that depression is over), such orientation understated the severity of the crisis.

Other domains show a more difficult situation:
- **employment rate fell** in 20 EU countries;
- **in all** 28 EU countries without exception share of gross investment in GDP decreased;
- **risk of poverty as percent of total population increased** in 24 EU countries;
- **income distribution worsened** as Gini coefficient and income quartile share ratio increased in 25 EU countries;
- **healthy life years at birth decreased** for males and females in 15-18 EU countries.

Please consult S-time-matrices for indicators 5, 7, 17, 19, 20, 22, and 23, where this is visually very easy to detect by comparing the latest years in bold against the values obtained in the whole analysed period. **This confirms the telling power of S-time-matrix** rearrangement of time series data by the levels of the indicators and times achieved to deliver a good summary overview with clear understanding to decision-makers as well as to the general public.

4. Life expectancy at birth and Human Development Index are two indicators that have shown continuous improvements over five and three decades, respectively. However, there are still large differences between EU countries for both of them. For these two indicators we have also prepared tables of S-time-distance as a novel measure of disparity and S-time-step as a novel descriptive measure of dynamics. For the life expectancy we selected the average of ten best countries in the world as benchmark; only three of the EU countries are higher than that international benchmark, five of them are lagging the benchmark by more than 30 years. For HDI the benchmark was the average of the very high human development group in the world; four EU countries were ahead of that, six at the bottom were lagging more than 20 years. S-time-step showed that 3.8 years were needed in recent past to increase one year of life expectancy, as an easily understandable description of dynamics complementing the growth rate measure.

5. This positive picture of dynamics in the two above indicators is followed by time matrices for **per capita GDP in PPS and median income in PPS**. The relative differences between the countries are very large, ratio between countries at the top and bottom for GDP per capita is about 2.7. For median income there was Austria at approximate level 20,000, on the one hand, and Romania with 3,000, on the other, showing a ratio of about 6.7 – a tremendous gap that can be analysed also for other countries. The time series are not long enough that similar S-time-distance time lags could be easily calculated for per capita GDP.

6. The material situation is accompanied with time matrix for **employment rate**, which again showed vast differences between EU countries. Furthermore, the most striking conclusion is the severity of fall of employment rate in the current crisis, which fell in 20 EU countries. It is the fall in the employment rate that shows better the magnitude of the blow of the financial crisis in developed world to the EU (and USA); the fall in the GDP per capita undervalues the severity of the current depression.

7. After employment rate as indicator of quantity input of human factor of production, the fall in **share of gross fixed investment** as an indicator of material input of one factor of production shows in a dramatic way at a glance the disastrous effects of the world financial system in the current depression on the GDP growth rates. **In all 28 EU countries** without exception the investment share decreased, for EU15 average and the USA for 3 steps. Ireland and Greece had the largest drops for even 13 steps (from share of 26 percent in 2007 to 13 percent in 2013).

8. R&D expenditure in GDP and summary innovation index illustrate the diversity and changes in these two indicators of quality improvement in some factors of production. Both indicators differ greatly among EU countries, the ratio between the highest and the lowest countries may vary from fivefold to threefold magnitude. Tertiary attainment indicates increase in this quality of human factor in all analysed countries.

9. The trend towards higher **share of the population aged 65 years or more in the total population** in the last five decades is very clear. Italy, Germany, and Greece already surpassed the 20 percent share. Eurostat prepared projections for the old age dependency ratio for the period 2013-2080. This time matrix is an example how projections over the period of 67 years and 28 countries can with some interpolations encompass potential 1876 entries over more than six decades in a compressed single one page table.

10. Persons killed in road accidents are showing continuous improvement but also very large differences among countries in the EU. At the same time 80-90 people per 1,000,000 inhabitants more are killed on roads in USA and Korea than in the best EU countries. For deaths due to homicide for Estonia, Lithuania, and Latvia their current values, though decreasing, are still very much higher than in other EU countries. Infant mortality rate is a story of enormous improvements in the last 50 years.

11. A set indicators tell a story about the situation with respect to the **risk of poverty, income inequality, and healthy life years** in EU countries, with special focus on changes in the current crisis. Unfortunately the conclusions are unanimous about the effects of world financial crisis on individual EU countries: risk of poverty as percent of total population increased in 24 EU countries; income distribution worsened as Gini coefficient and income quartile share ratio increased in 25 EU countries; healthy life years at birth decreased for males and females in 15-18 EU countries.

12. In the broadly discussed information and communication domain trends were favourable. For **household with broadband access and regular Internet use** extremely high dynamics was observed. Also scientific publications per million inhabitants showed good performance in scientific domain. Percent of early leavers from education and training decreased though there were still large differences between countries.

13. Two indicators addressed some elements of environment domain. For **share of energy from renewable sources**, apart from the exceptional share in Sweden, the range between countries is very wide from a few percent to more than 30 percent of the renewable sources, which will be a challenge for the general EU orientation towards more renewable sources. **Urban population exposure to air pollution by particulate matter PM10** is indicating the difficult challenge in this respect as in the recent years only seven EU countries are at the WHO recommended annual level of 20 micrograms per cubic metre or lower, 21 EU countries are not meeting such recommendation.

14. Proportion of seats in national parliaments held by women again shows an example of very wide country differences in a social domain, from 10 to 46 percent. The time matrix presentation and visualisation for gender disparities in this indicator makes it very easy to understand and can be used for other indicators describing the share of women in several fields, like employment, women in science, etc.

15. The voyage through 30 time matrices for 28 countries compressed a very large amount of data, expressing multidimensional nature of development and well-being, indicating both visually and in numbers that **very large differences exist between EU countries with respects to levels and dynamics**. Using the innovative approach of time distance methodology the telling power of **S-time-matrix provided a good summary overview at-a-glance over many domains with clear understanding to decision-makers as well as to the general public.** Seeing with new eyes creates new knowledge and better understanding.

REFERENCES

ARRS (2014). Time Matrix for Publications per Million Inhabitants in 5-year Periods, based on ISI database Web of Science, 2013. https://www.arrs.gov.si/en/analize/odlicnost/objave1.asp.

EC (2013). Innovation Union Scoreboard 2013, Annex E. Belgium.

Eurostat (2014). Eurostat database http://epp.eurostat.ec.europa.eu/portal/page/portal/eurostat/home.

OECD (2013). OECDStatExtracts, http://stats.oecd.org/.

Sicherl, P. (2011a). New Understanding and Insights from Time-Series Data Based on Two Generic Measures: S-Time-Distance and S-Time-Step. OECD Statistics Working Papers. 2011/09. OECD Publishing. http://dx.doi.org/10.1787/5kg1zpzzl1tg-en.

Sicherl, P. (2011b). 50 years of OECD countries at a glance, SICENTER, Ljubljana, January 19.

Sicherl, P. (2012). Time Distance in Economics and Statistics, New Insights from Existing Data, pp 444. Edition echoraum, Wien.

Sicherl, P. (2013). A geek's guide to measuring the MDGs, The Guardian, web page http://www.guardian.co.uk/global-development-professionals-network/2013/feb/28/measuring-mdgs.

Sicherl, P. (2014a). World Inequalities in Human Development Index (1980-2012), Printed by CreateSpace, Charleston SC.

Sicherl, P. (2014b). World inequalities in the Human Development Index (1980-2012) - Time Distance View, ProgBlog, wikiprogress. http://theblogprogress.blogspot.com/2014/03/world-inequalities-in-human-development.html.

Sicherl, P. (2014c). Inter-temporal Aspect of Well-Being. In: Michalos AC (Ed.). Encyclopedia of Quality of Life and Well-Being Research. Springer, Dordrecht, Netherlands: Springer, p. 3353-3363.

Sicherl, P. (2014d). How Much Longer Live Women Than Men Around the Globe? Astonishing Differences between Countries, Printed by CreateSpace, Charleston SC.

UN (2011). Department of Economic and Social Affairs, Population Division, World Population Prospects: The 2010 Revision, CD-ROM Edition.

UNDP (2013). Human Development Report 2013, The Rise of the South: Human Progress in a Diverse World, New York.

ANNEX

A1 Time Matrix Calculator to calculate time matrix for your own data

Example of input file
(for indicator life expectancy at birth)

Life expectancy at birth	1990	1991	1992	1993	1994	1995	1996	1997	1998	1999	2000	2001	2002	2003	2004	2005	2006	2007	2008	2009	2010	2011	2012
Belgium	76.2	76.3	76.5	76.5	76.8	77.0	77.3	77.5	77.6	77.7	77.9	78.1	78.2	78.3	79.0	79.1	79.5	79.9	79.8	80.1	80.3	80.7	80.5
Bulgaria	71.2	71.1	71.2	71.2	70.9	71.0	70.8	70.3	70.9	71.6	71.6	71.9	72.1	72.3	72.5	72.7	73.0	73.3	73.7	73.8	74.2	74.4	
Czech Republic	71.5	72.0	72.4	72.9	73.2	73.3	74.0	74.1	74.7	74.9	75.1	75.3	75.4	75.3	75.9	76.1	76.7	77.0	77.3	77.4	77.7	78.0	78.1
Denmark	74.9	75.3	75.3	75.2	75.5	75.5	75.7	76.1	76.5	76.6	76.9	77.0	77.1	77.4	78.3	78.4	78.4	78.8	79.0	79.3	79.9	80.2	
Germany	75.4	75.7	76.2	76.2	76.6	76.7	77.0	77.4	77.8	78.0	78.3	78.6	78.6	78.6	79.3	79.4	79.9	80.1	80.2	80.3	80.5	80.6	81.0
Estonia	69.9	69.8	69.1	68.1	66.6	67.7	69.9	70.1	69.7	70.6	71.1	70.9	71.4	71.9	72.4	73.0	73.2	73.2	74.4	75.3	76.0	76.6	76.7
Ireland	74.8	75.0	75.4	75.3	75.8	75.5	75.8	76.0	76.2	76.1	76.6	77.2	77.7	78.2	78.6	79.0	79.3	79.7	80.2	80.2	80.8	80.9	
Greece	77.1	77.1	77.0	77.4	77.5	77.5	77.6	77.9	77.9	77.9	78.2	78.8	79.0	79.1	79.3	79.5	79.8	79.7	80.2	80.4	80.6	80.8	80.7
Spain	77.0	77.1	77.6	77.7	78.1	78.1	78.2	78.7	78.8	78.8	79.3	79.8	79.8	79.7	80.4	80.3	81.1	81.1	81.5	81.9	82.4	82.6	82.5
France	77.0	77.2	77.5	77.5	78.0	78.1	78.2	78.6	78.8	78.9	79.2	79.3	79.4	79.3	80.4	80.4	81.0	81.3	81.4	81.6	81.9	82.3	82.1
Croatia													74.6	74.7	74.6	75.3	75.9	75.8	76.0	76.3	76.7	77.2	77.3
Italy	77.1	77.1	77.5	77.8	78.0	78.3	78.7	79.0	79.1	79.6	79.9	80.3	80.4	80.1	80.9	80.9	81.4	81.6	81.7	81.8	82.2	82.4	82.4
Cyprus			77.2	77.1	77.4	77.7	77.4	77.2	78.0	77.7	79.0	78.7	79.0	79.1	78.7	80.1	79.8	80.6	81.0	81.5	81.2	81.1	
Latvia													70.2	70.6	70.9	70.6	70.6	70.8	72.1	72.8	73.1	73.9	74.1
Lithuania	71.5	70.6	70.5	69.0	68.6	69.1	70.3	71.1	71.4	71.8	72.1	71.6	72.0	72.0	71.2	71.0	70.7	71.7	72.9	73.3	73.7	74.1	
Luxembourg	75.7	75.7	75.3	76.0	76.7	76.8	76.8	77.1	77.3	78.0	78.0	78.0	78.1	77.9	79.2	79.6	79.4	79.5	80.7	80.8	80.8	81.1	81.5
Hungary	69.4	69.4	69.2	69.2	69.6	70.0	70.6	71.1	71.0	71.1	71.9	72.5	72.6	72.6	73.0	73.0	73.5	73.6	74.2	74.4	74.7	75.1	75.3
Malta								77.2	77.3	77.4	77.5	77.4	78.4	78.9	78.8	78.7	79.4	79.4	79.5	79.9	79.7	80.4	80.9
Netherlands	77.1	77.2	77.4	77.1	77.6	77.6	77.6	77.6	78.0	78.1	78.0	78.2	78.4	78.6	79.0	79.3	79.6	80.0	80.4	80.5	80.9	81.0	81.3
Austria	75.8	75.9	76.1	76.3	76.7	76.9	77.1	77.5	77.9	77.9	78.3	78.8	78.9	78.9	79.3	79.6	79.5	80.1	80.4	80.6	80.5	80.8	81.1
Poland	70.7	70.4	71.0	71.5	71.8	72.0	72.3	72.7	73.1	73.1	73.8	74.2	74.5	74.7	74.9	75.0	75.3	75.4	75.6	75.9	76.4	76.9	76.9
Portugal	74.1	74.1	74.7	74.6	75.2	75.4	75.3	75.8	76.0	76.2	76.8	77.2	77.4	77.8	78.2	79.0	79.3	79.7	80.1	80.7	80.6		
Romania	69.9	70.1	69.5	69.5	69.4	69.3	68.8	69.1	69.9	70.6	71.2	71.1	71.0	71.4	71.9	72.2	72.8	73.3	73.5	73.6	73.8	74.6	74.5
Slovenia	73.9	73.6	73.7	73.6	74.0	74.7	75.2	75.2	75.3	75.7	76.2	76.4	76.6	76.4	77.4	77.5	78.3	78.1	79.1	79.4	79.8	80.1	80.6
Slovakia	71.1	71.1	71.5	72.0	72.5	72.4	72.9	72.9	72.8	73.2	73.3	73.6	73.8	73.8	74.2	74.1	74.5	74.6	74.9	75.3	75.6	76.1	76.3
Finland	75.1	75.5	75.7	75.9	76.7	76.7	77.0	77.2	77.4	77.6	77.8	78.2	78.3	78.6	79.0	79.1	79.5	79.6	79.9	80.1	80.2	80.6	80.7
Sweden	77.7	77.8	78.2	78.2	78.9	79.0	79.2	79.4	79.5	79.6	79.8	79.9	80.0	80.3	80.7	81.0	81.1	81.3	81.5	81.6	81.9	81.8	
United Kingdom			76.2	76.8	76.7	77.0	77.2	77.4	77.5	78.0	78.2	78.3	78.4	79.0	79.2	79.5	79.7	79.8	80.4	80.6	81.0	81.0	

Source: Eurostat, Life expectancy by age and sex, Total [demo_mlexpec].

Available software tool:
Time Matrix Calculator

Faculty of Social Sciences, University of Ljubljana and SICENTER, Ljubljana, Slovenia

Methodology: Professor Pavle Sicherl
Programming: May Doušak
Testing: Jaka Hajnšek

www.timedistance.net

Time matrix for life expectancy at birth

LEVEL	67	68	69	70	71	72	73	74	75	76	77	78	79	80	81	82
Spain											1990	1994	1999	2003	2006	**2009**
Italy												1994	1997	2000	2005	2010
France											1990	1994	1999	2004	2006	2010
Sweden													1992	1995	2002	**2006**
Cyprus													2000	2005	2007	**2009**
Netherlands													1999	2004	2006	**2010**
Austria											1992	1996	1999	2003	2006	**2011**
Luxembourg											1993	1997	2003	2004	2007	**2011**
Malta													2000	2003	2008	**2011**
United Kingdom												1996	2000	2004	**2012**	
Germany											1992	1996	1999	2004	2007	**2012**
Greece												1992	1999	2002	**2008**	
Ireland								1991			1997	2001	2003	2005	**2008**	
Finland											1993	1996	2001	2004	**2009**	
Belgium												1995	2001	2004	**2009**	
Portugal										1993	1998	2001	2004	2006	**2010**	
Slovenia									1994		1996	2000	2004	2006	2008	**2011**
Denmark											1990	1997	2001	2004	2009	**2011**
Czech Republic								1991	1993	1996	2000	2005	2007	**2011**		
Croatia										2004	2008	**2011**				
Poland					1992	1995	1998	2001	2005	**2009**						
Estonia	1994	1995	1996	1998	2001	2003	2005	2008	2009	**2010**						
Slovakia						1993	1999	2004	2008	**2011**						
Hungary				1995	1998	2000	2005	2008	**2011**							
Romania				1997	1998	2002	2004	2006	**2010**							
Bulgaria						1998	2002	2007	**2011**							
Latvia						2007	2008	2010	**2012**							
Lithuania				1995	1996	2007	2008	2009	**2012**							

Required format of the input file:
Input file is an Excel file with data table in active sheet.
In the row 1 there are time units (number format) from cell B1 to the right; in the column A are unit names (text format, e.g., countries, regions, etc.) from cell A2 down.

Time matrix condenses information over many units and years (from about 550 entries in the input file), into much smaller number of about 140 entries, **which is a great advantage for presentation and visualisation providing a good summary overview of the situation at a glance**.

The year presented in **bold** show the latest presented year of the indicator for the given country. It can help to quickly observe whether there was a noticeable decrease in later years in the observed period.

A2 How to learn the time distance methodology

For methodology see freely available paper by Statistics Directorate, OECD:
P. Sicherl, New Understanding and Insights from Time-Series Data Based on Two Generic Measures: S-time-distance and S-time-step; Working paper No. 44, Statistics Directorate, OECD Publishing, Paris, November 2011.
Please download the paper on http://dx.doi.org/10.1787/5kg1zpzzl1tg-en.

More detailed methodological issues and numerous applications are available in the book:
Pavle Sicherl, Time Distance in Economics and Statistics, New Insights from Existing Data, p. 444, Echoraum, Vienna, 2012.
More information about the book is available on wikiprogress,
http://www.wikiprogress.org/index.php/Time_Distance_in_Economics_and_Statistics.

The book is available on amazon.de,
http://www.amazon.de/gp/product/3901941274.

Brief definition of two novel statistical measures: S-time-distance and S-time-step

The statistical measure **S-time-distance** measures the distance (proximity) in time between the points in time when the two series compared reach a specified level of the indicator X. For instance, S-time-matrix for indicator 1 earlier showed that life expectancy of about 81 years was reached in the United Kingdom in 2012; this level was reached by the international frontier in 2006, with S-time-distance lead of 6 years or lag of 6 years for the UK. **S-time-distance** for a given level of X_L is defined as:

$$S_{ij} (X_L) = \Delta t (X_L) = t_i (X_L) - t_j (X_L) \qquad (1)$$

The **S-time-step** measures the time elapsed between two levels of a time series, providing an alternative description of its growth rate, measuring the growth of a series by using the inverse relation to the conventional $\Delta X / \Delta t$ growth rate metrics. For instance, the values of S-time-step in matrix 1b showed that the number of years needed in the past to reach the next consecutive level of life expectancy for EU28 was 3.8 years. This means nearly 4 years were needed for increase of one year of life expectancy from level of 79 to the level of 80 years. In the usual way of expressing dynamics in percentage terms this change would be expressed as change of about 1% over these years or 0.3% growth rate per year. Both statistical measures add information. Both measures, 3.8 years and/or 0.3% growth rate per year, are valid descriptions of the dynamics of change, while for general public S-time-step might be even easier to understand. **S-time-step** is expressed in units of time and is defined as:

$$S_i (\Delta X_L) = [t_i (X_L+\Delta X) - t_i (X_L)]/\Delta X \qquad (2)$$

In graphical terms, the usual way to compare time series is to look at the vertical dimension, i.e. for a given point in time. The time distance approach provides an additional perspective, comparing time series in the horizontal dimension, i.e. for a given level of the variable. The S-time-distance approach has two advantages: first, expressed in time units, it is easy to understand by policymakers, professionals, managers, media and the general public; second, time distance can be compared across variables, fields of concern, and units of comparison.

Gender disparities in life expectancy at birth, EU27 average in 2010: static index and time distance

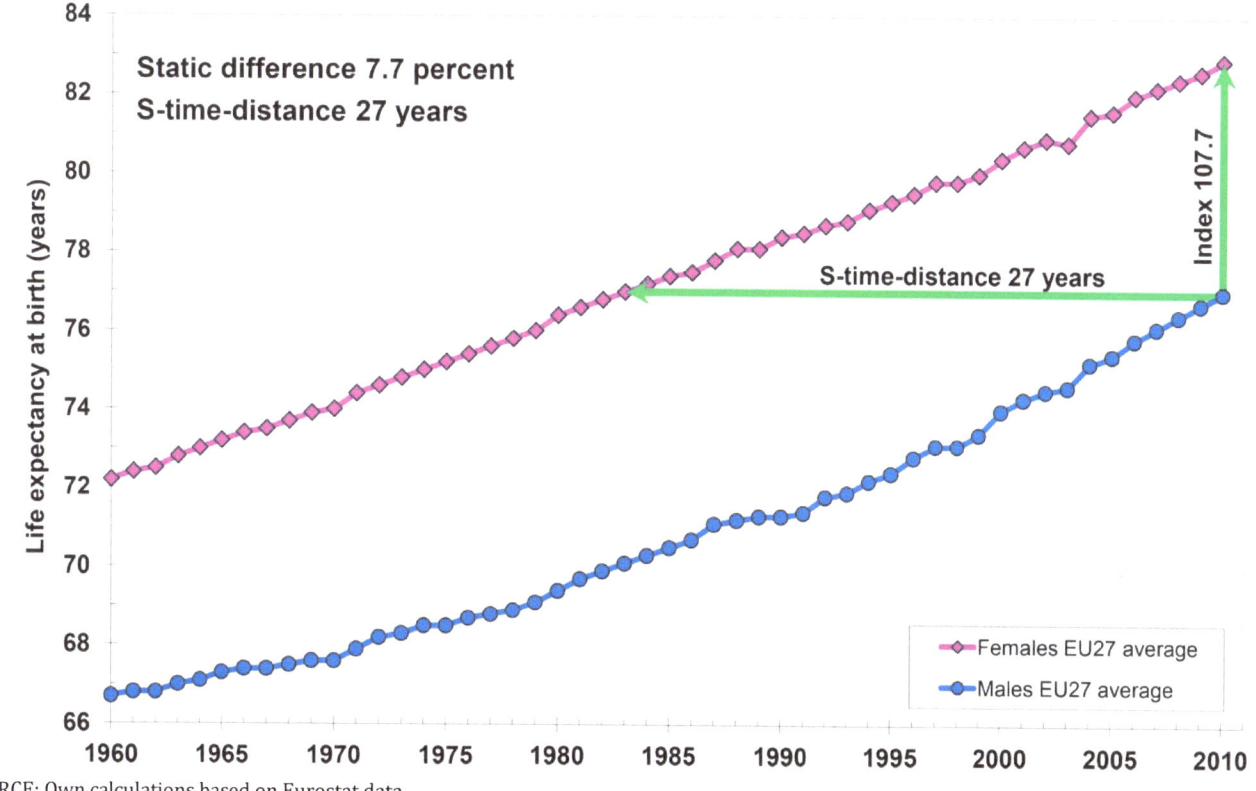

SOURCE: Own calculations based on Eurostat data.

Time series can be compared in two dimensions, in the figure above we present the example of the gender disparities in life expectancy at birth for EU27 aggregates. One way is to compare time series at the given point in time, i.e. in our case the static gap in life expectancy between women and men in

2010. The absolute difference amounts to 5.9 years; the index is 107.7. Another dimension of the degree of disparity is taking into consideration the distance in years when men and women reached the same reference level of the variable, in our case the life expectancy for men in 2010 was reached by women already in 1983 (i.e. 27 years earlier): S-time-distance amounted to 27 years.

Since time distance view provides an additional dimension of temporal disparity between two time series, results by other methods are left unchanged but new conclusions can be reached.

A3 Data sources

	Indicators	Source	Code of the dataset or table
1	Life expectancy at birth	Eurostat (2014)	demo_mlexpec
2	Human Development Index	UNDP (2013)	http://hdr.undp.org, Data Annex
3	GDP per capita in PPS	Eurostat (2014)	prc_ppp_ind
4	Median income in PPS	Eurostat (2014)	ilc_di03
5	Employment rate (15 to 64 years)	Eurostat (2014)	lfsi_emp_a
6	Activity rate (15 to 64 years)	Eurostat (2014)	lfsi_act_a
7	Share of gross fixed investment in GDP	Eurostat (2014)	nama_gdp_k
8	R&D expenditure (GERD), percent of GDP	Eurostat (2014)	rd_e_gerdtot
9	Summary Innovation Index	EC (2013)	Annex E, SII time series
10	Tertiary attainment for age group 15-64	Eurostat (2014)	edat_lfse_07
11	Proportion of population aged 65 years and more	Eurostat (2014)	demo_pjanind
12	Old age dependency ratio, projections 2013-2080	Eurostat (2014)	tsdde511
13	Population growth rates, total	Eurostat (2014)	demo_pjanbroad
14	Persons killed in road accidents per million inhabitants	Eurostat (2014)	tran_sf_roadse, demo_pjanbroad
15	Death due to homicide, standardised death rate	Eurostat (2014)	hlth_cd_asdr
16	Infant mortality rate	Eurostat (2014)	demo_minfind
17	At-risk-of-poverty (percent of total population)	Eurostat (2014)	ilc_li02
18	At-risk-of-poverty (percent of elderly population)	Eurostat (2014)	ilc_li02
19	Income quintile share ratio S80/S20	Eurostat (2014)	ilc_di11
20	GINI coefficient	Eurostat (2014)	ilc_di12
21	Early leavers from education and training	Eurostat (2014)	edat_lfse_14
22	Healthy life years at birth - females	Eurostat (2014)	hlth_hlye_h, hlth_hlye
23	Healthy life years at birth - males	Eurostat (2014)	hlth_hlye_h, hlth_hlye
24	Households with broadband access	Eurostat (2014)	isoc_pibi_hba
25	Regular Internet use	Eurostat (2014)	isoc_ci_ifp_fu
26	Share of energy from renewable sources	Eurostat (2014)	nrg_ind_335a
27	Urban population exposure to air pollution by PM10	Eurostat (2014)	env_air_ind
28	Publications per million inhabitants	ARRS (2014)	based on ISI database Web of Science, 2013
29	Proportion of seats in parliaments held by women	OECD (2013)	Employment, Proportion of seats by women
30	Current account balance in percent of GDP	Eurostat (2014)	tipsbp20

ABOUT THE AUTHOR

Professor Pavle Sicherl, Founder of SICENTER and principal researcher, 1993-present, Professor of Economics, University of Ljubljana, Slovenia (1975-2003); macroeconomic adviser in the Harvard University Development Advisory Service team in Ethiopia, (1970-1974); in 1960's Deputy Director of the Yugoslav Institute of Economic Research in Belgrade.

Born in Ljubljana, Ph.D. (economics) and Dipl.Econ., University of Ljubljana; M.A. Development Economics (Williams College, MA, USA). Speciality: growth and inequality, he introduced new statistical measures, S-time-distance and S-time-step, to amend the present methods of analysing time series data and disparities in many fields.

For this idea he received many fellowships and invitations: Senior Fulbright Research Award (Yale), London School of Economics, Institute of World Economics (Kiel), Institute for Advanced Studies (Vienna), etc. Visiting professor abroad, project leader for international and national projects, and consultant to the World Bank, OECD, UN, ILO, UNIDO, INSTRAW, ITU, EUROCHAMBRES.

Biography: Who's Who in the World, Marquis, 1991-1992 ... 2013.

Website: www.gaptimer.eu

Email: pavle.sicherl@gaptimer.eu